FOR ORGANS, PIANOS & ELECTRONIC KEYBOARDS

E-Z PLAY TODAY

277

STEVIE WONDER GREATEST HITS

CONTENTS

2	Boogie On Reggae Woman
4	Do I Do
8	Don't You Worry 'Bout a Thing
14	For Once in My Life
11	Go Home
16	Heaven Help Us All
30	Higher Ground
20	I Just Called to Say I Love You
24	I Wish
28	If You Really Love Me
33	Living for the City
36	Love Light in Flight
40	My Cherie Amour
42	Overjoyed
45	Part Time Lover
50	A Place in the Sun
52	Ribbon in the Sky
56	Send One Your Love
59	Signed, Sealed, Delivered I'm Yours
64	Sir Duke
62	Superstition
67	That Girl
70	Uptight (Everything's Alright)
74	Yester-Me, Yester-You, Yesterday
76	You Are the Sunshine of My Life
78	You Haven't Done Nothin'

ISBN 978-0-634-06660-3

HAL•LEONARD®
CORPORATION
7777 W. BLUEMOUND RD. P.O. BOX 13819 MILWAUKEE, WI 53213

In Australia Contact:
Hal Leonard Australia Pty. Ltd.
22 Taunton Drive P.O. Box 5130
Cheltenham East, 3192 Victoria, Australia
Email: ausadmin@halleonard.com

For all works contained herein:
Unauthorized copying, arranging, adapting, recording or public performance is an infringement of copyright.
Infringers are liable under the law.

E-Z PLAY® TODAY Music Notation © 1975 by HAL LEONARD CORPORATION

E-Z PLAY and EASY ELECTRONIC KEYBOARD MUSIC are registered trademarks of HAL LEONARD CORPORATION.

Visit Hal Leonard Online at
www.halleonard.com

Boogie On Reggae Woman

Registration 2
Rhythm: Rock or Reggae

Words and Music by
Stevie Wonder

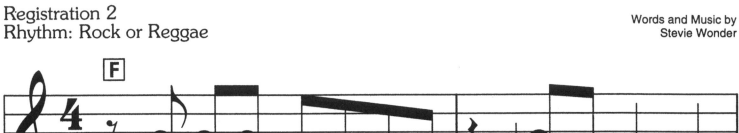

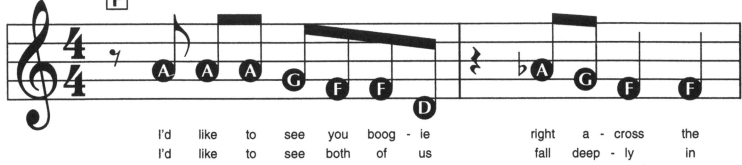

I'd like to see you boog - ie right a - cross the
I'd like to see both of us fall deep - ly in

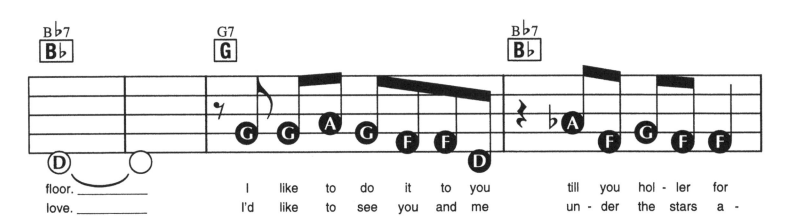

floor. _____ I like to do it to you till you hol - ler for
love. _____ I'd like to see you and me un - der the stars a -

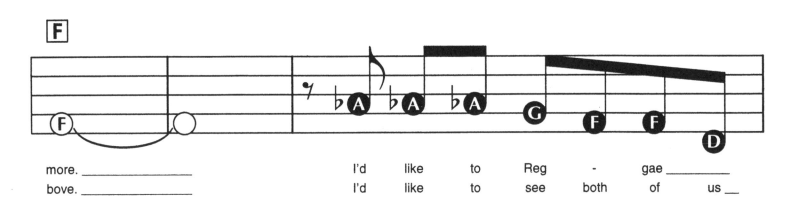

more. _____ I'd like to Reg - gae _____
bove. _____ I'd like to see both of us __

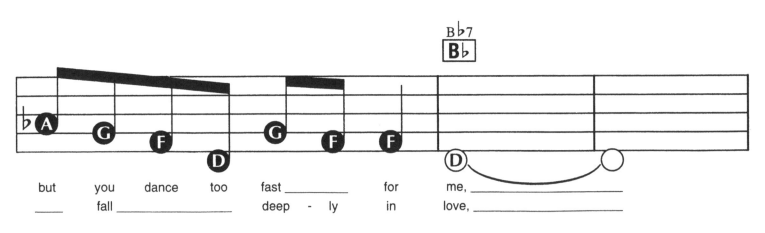

but you dance too fast _____ for me, _____
____ fall _____ deep - ly in love, _____

© 1974 (Renewed 2002) JOBETE MUSIC CO., INC. and BLACK BULL MUSIC
c/o EMI APRIL MUSIC INC.
All Rights Reserved   International Copyright Secured   Used by Permission

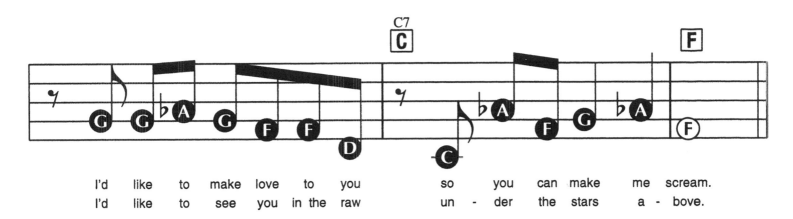

I'd like to make love to you so you can make me scream.
I'd like to see you in the raw un - der the stars a - bove.

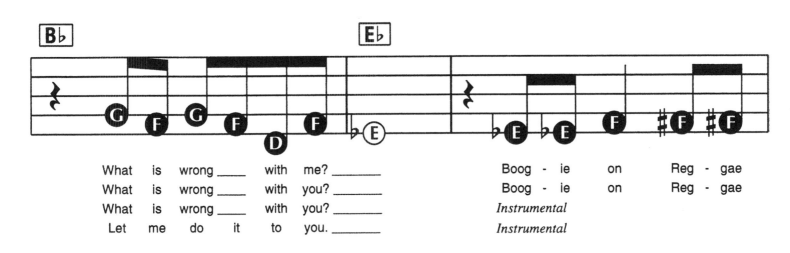

Boog - ie on Reg - gae wom - an,
Boog - ie on Reg - gae wom - an,
Instrumental
Instrumental

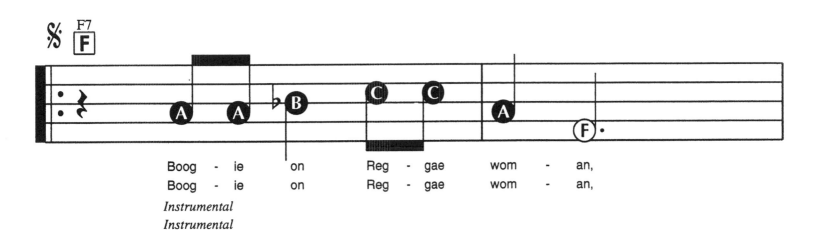

What is wrong ____ with me? _____
What is wrong ____ with you? _____
What is wrong ____ with you? _____
Let me do it to you. _____

Boog - ie on Reg - gae
Boog - ie on Reg - gae
Instrumental
Instrumental

1st time, return to beginning; 2nd time repeat from % 4 times and fade

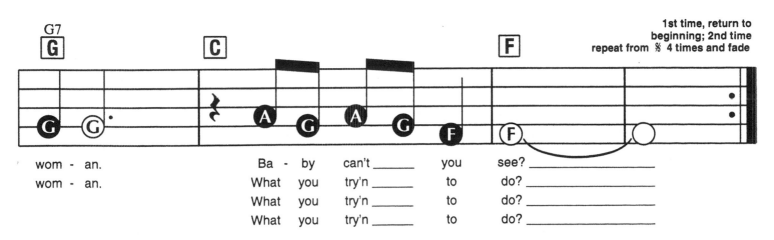

wom - an.
wom - an.

Ba - by can't ____ you see? _____
What you try'n ____ to do? _____
What you try'n ____ to do? _____
What you try'n ____ to do? _____

Do I Do

Registration 1
Rhythm: 16 Beat, Funk or Disco

Words and Music by
Stevie Wonder

© 1982 JOBETE MUSIC CO., INC. and BLACK BULL MUSIC
c/o EMI APRIL MUSIC INC.
All Rights Reserved   International Copyright Secured   Used by Permission

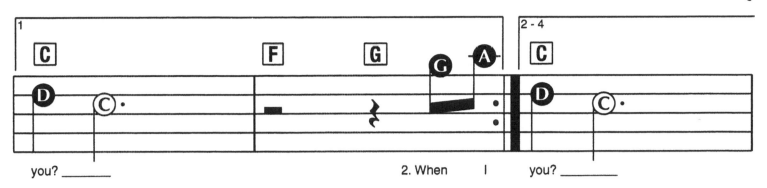

you? _____ 2. When I you? _____

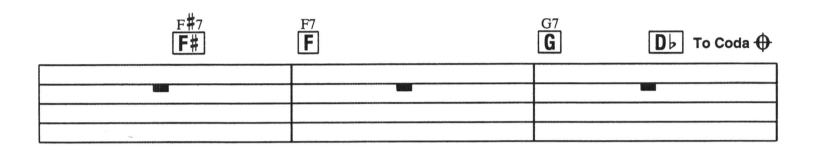

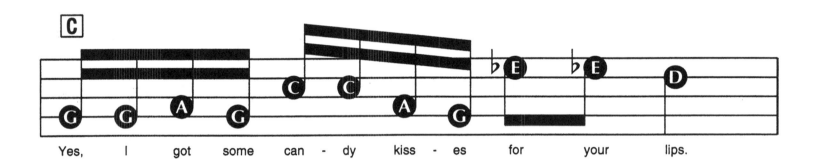

Yes, I got some can - dy kiss - es for your lips.

Yes, I got some hon - ey - suck - le choc - 'late drip - pin' kiss - es full of

love _____ for you.

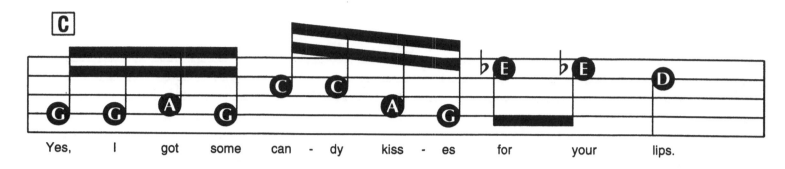

Yes, I got some can - dy kiss - es for your lips.

Yes, I got some hon - ey - suck - le choc - 'late drip - pin' kiss - es full of

love _____ for you.   My life has been wait - ing for your

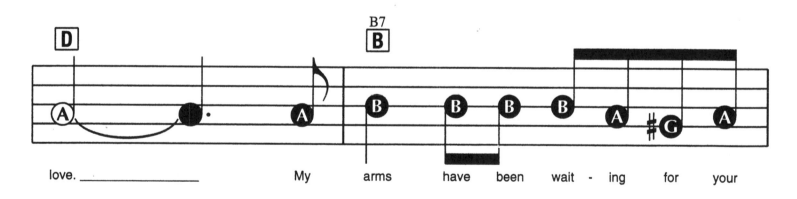

love. _____   My arms have been wait - ing for your

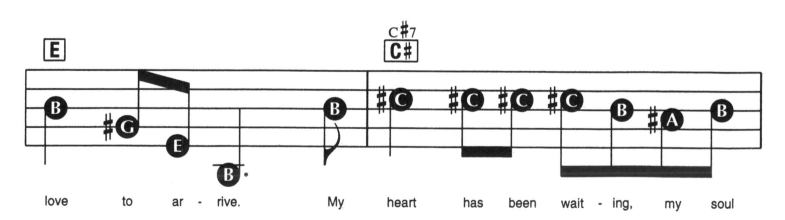

love to ar - rive.   My heart has been wait - ing, my soul

1st time Return to 𝄋
2nd time D.S. al Coda
(Return to 𝄋
Play to ⊕ and
Skip to coda)

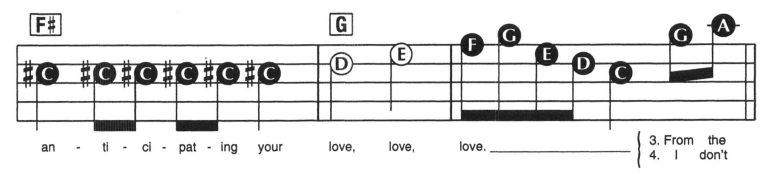

an - ti - ci - pat - ing your love, love, love. _____
3. From the
4. I don't

CODA ⊕

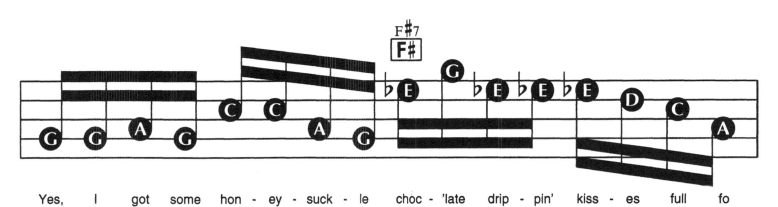

Yes, I got some can - dy kiss - es for your lips.

F#7

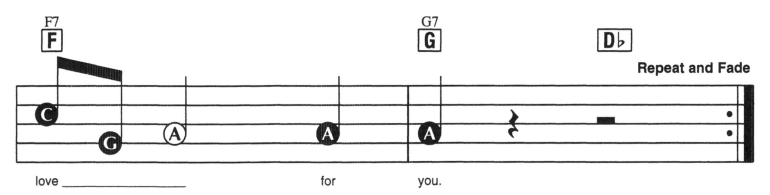

Yes, I got some hon - ey - suck - le choc - 'late drip - pin' kiss - es full fo

F7   G7   **Repeat and Fade**

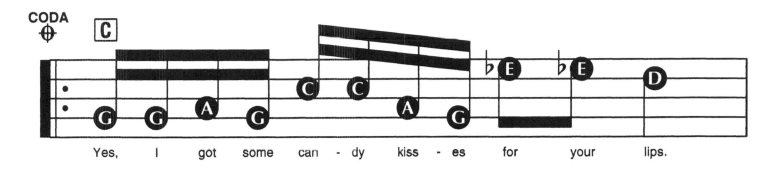

love _____ for you.

Additional Lyrics

2. When I hear you on the phone,
Your sweet sexy voice turns my ear all the way on.
Just the mention of your name
Seems to drive my head insane.
Girl, do I do ...etc.

3. From the time that I awake
I'm imagining the good love that we'll make.
If to me your vibe can do all this
Just imagine how it's gonna feel when we hug and kiss.
Sugar, do I do ...etc.

4. I don't care how long it might take,
'Cause I know the woman for me - you I'll make.
'Cause I will not deny myself the chance
Of being part of what feels like the right romance.
Girl, do I do ...etc.

Don't You Worry 'Bout a Thing

Registration 4
Rhythm: Latin

Words and Music by
Stevie Wonder

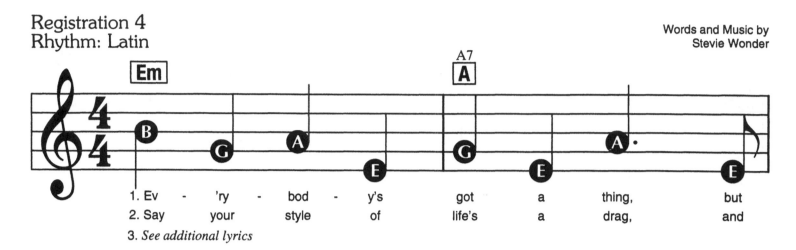

1. Ev - 'ry - bod - y's got a thing, but
2. Say your style of life's a drag, and
3. *See additional lyrics*

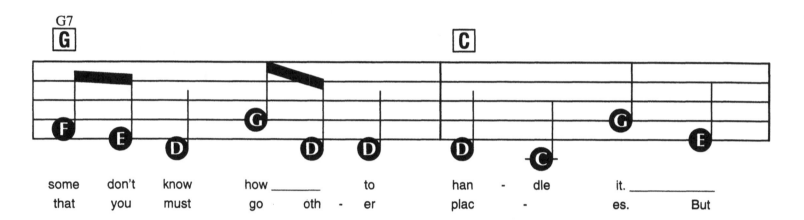

some don't know how _____ to han - dle it. _____
that you must go oth - er plac - es. But

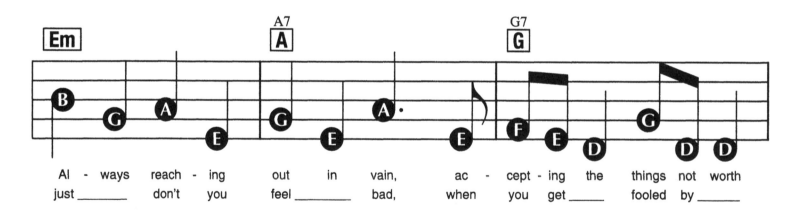

Al - ways reach - ing out in vain, ac - cept - ing the things not worth
just _____ don't you feel _____ bad, when you get _____ fooled by _____

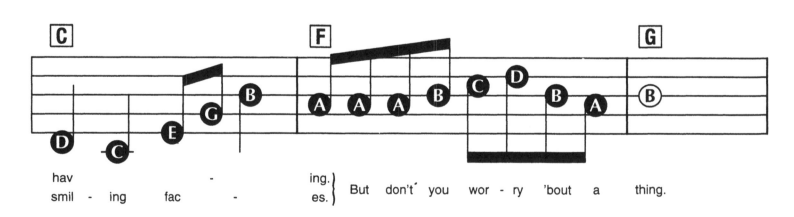

hav - ing.
smil - ing fac - es. But don't you wor - ry 'bout a thing.

© 1973 (Renewed 2001) JOBETE MUSIC CO., INC. and BLACK BULL MUSIC
c/o EMI APRIL MUSIC INC.
All Rights Reserved   International Copyright Secured   Used by Permission

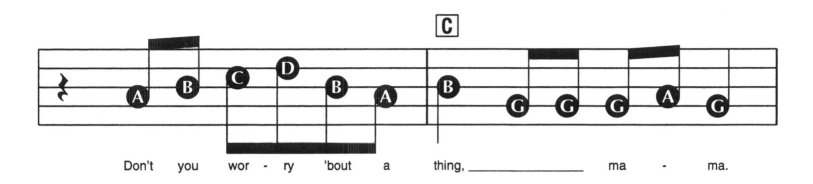

Don't you wor - ry 'bout a thing, _____ ma - ma.

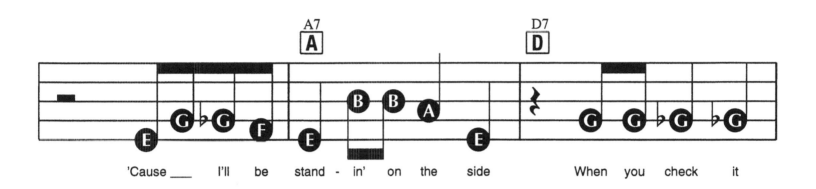

'Cause ___ I'll be stand - in' on the side   When you check it

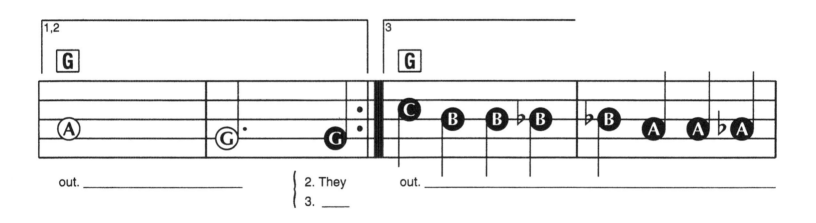

out. _____   { 2. They   out. _____

3. ____

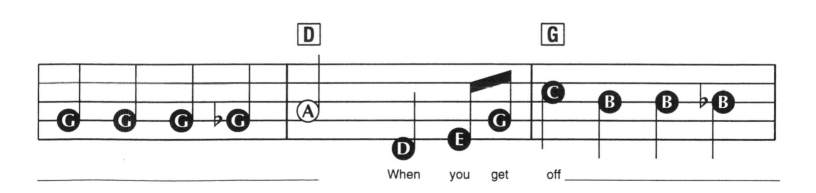

When you get off _____

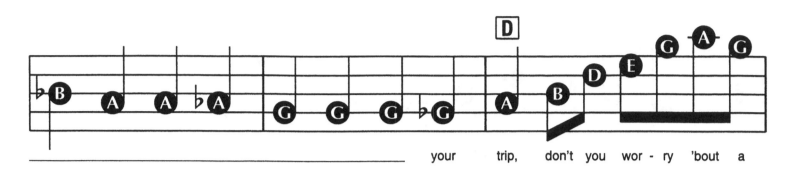

your trip, don't you wor - ry 'bout a

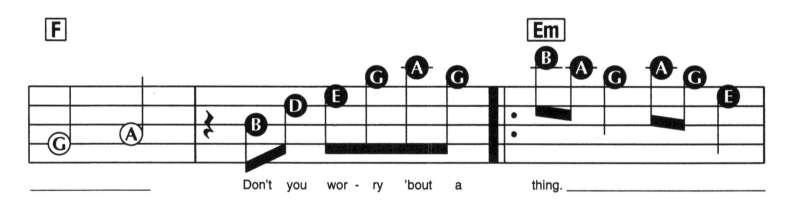

thing.

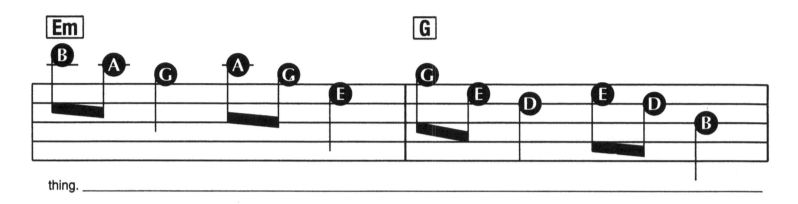

Don't you wor - ry 'bout a thing.

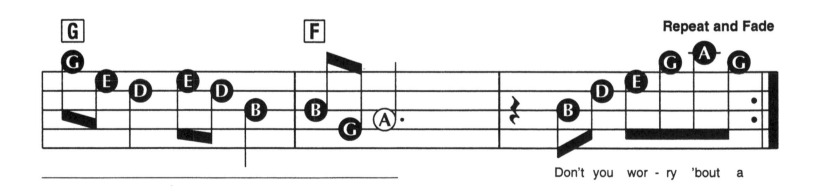

Repeat and Fade

Don't you wor - ry 'bout a

Additional Lyrics

3. Ev'rybody needs a change,
A chance to check out the new.
But you're the only one to see
The changes you take yourself through.
Don't you worry 'bout a thing,
Don't you worry 'bout a thing, pretty mama,
'Cause I'll be standin' in the wings
When you check it out.

Go Home

Registration 8
Rhythm: Samba

Words and Music by
Stevie Wonder

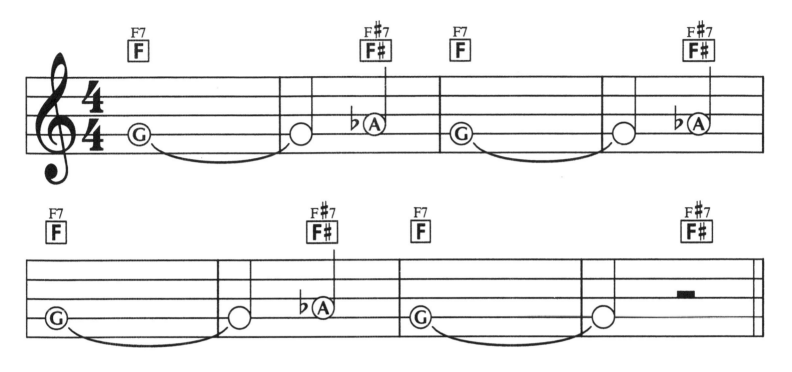

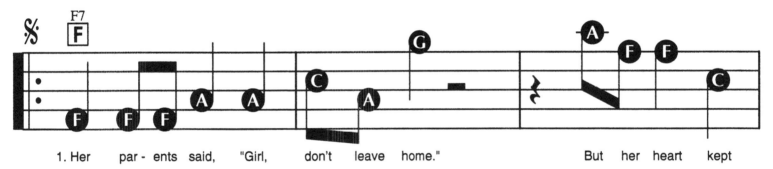

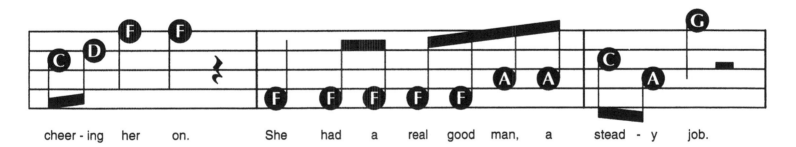

1. Her par - ents said, "Girl, don't leave home." But her heart kept
2, 3. *See additional lyrics*

cheer - ing her on. She had a real good man, a stead - y job.

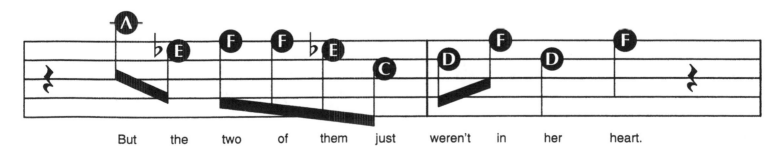

But the two of them just weren't in her heart.

© 1983 JOBETE MUSIC CO., INC. and BLACK BULL MUSIC
c/o EMI APRIL MUSIC INC.
All Rights Reserved   International Copyright Secured   Used by Permission

Chorus

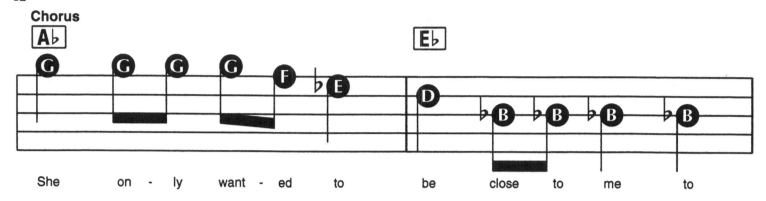

She on-ly want-ed to be close to me to

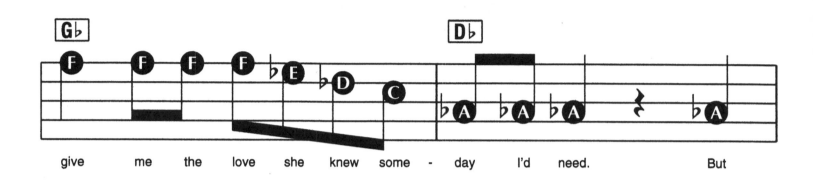

give me the love she knew some-day I'd need. But

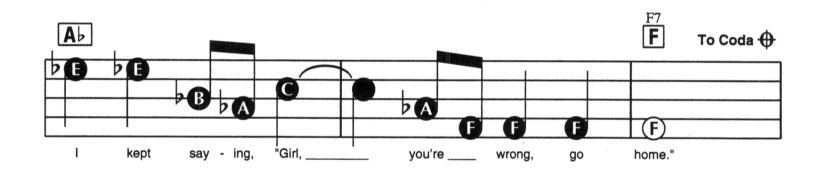

I kept say-ing, "Girl, _____ you're ____ wrong, go home."

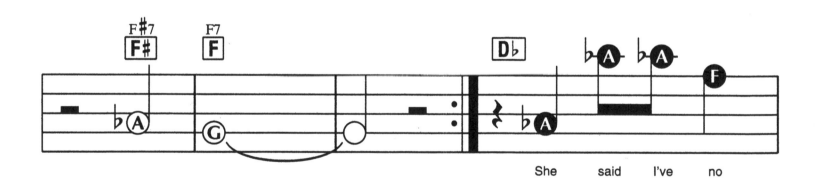

She said I've no

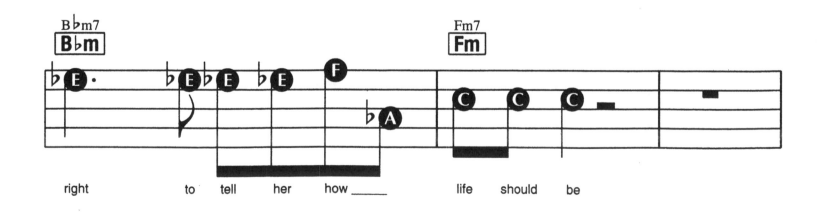

right to tell her how ____ life should be

13

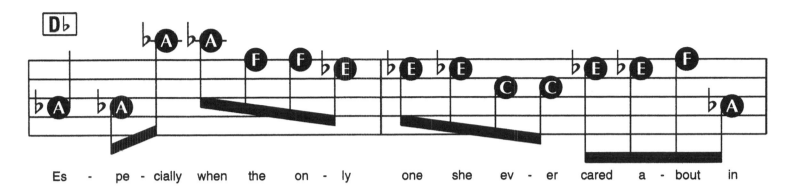

Es - pe - cially when the on - ly one she ev - er cared a - bout in

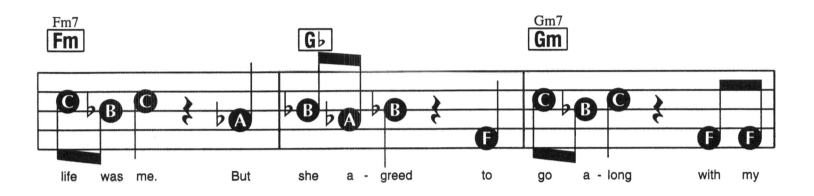

life was me. But she a - greed to go a - long with my

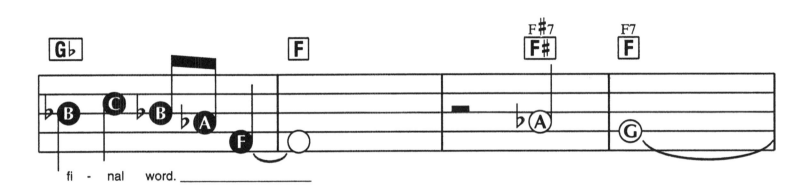

fi - nal word. _____

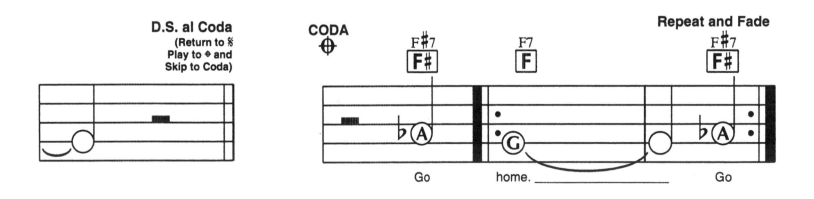

D.S. al Coda
(Return to %
Play to ⊕ and
Skip to Coda)

CODA

Repeat and Fade

Go home. _____ Go

Additional Lyrics

2. Long days, short nights when you're on the road.
   For a pretty girl it's a heavy load.
   And even so who'll pay your fare?
   She said, "I'll make it on a wing and a prayer."
   Chorus:

3. As fate would have life come around,
   My world started tumblin' down.
   I lost my family, my friends and job
   And set free the only one
   Who stuck with me from the start.
   Chorus:

For Once in My Life

Registration 8
Rhythm: Rock or Pops

Words by Ronald Miller
Music by Orlando Murden

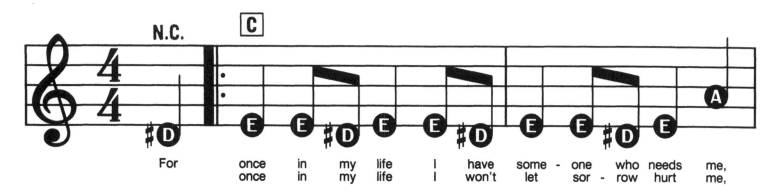

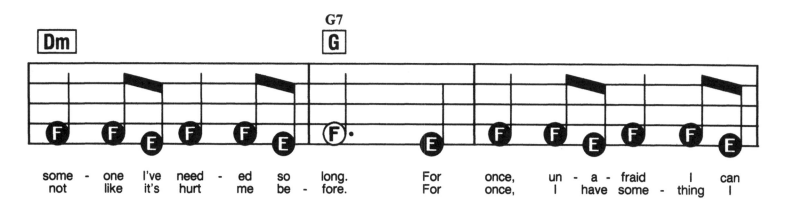

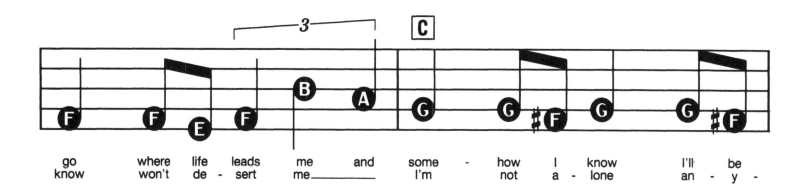

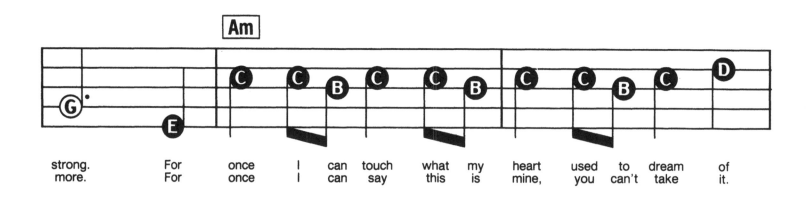

© 1965 (Renewed 1993) JOBETE MUSIC CO., INC. and STONE DIAMOND MUSIC CORP.
All Rights Controlled and Administered by EMI APRIL MUSIC INC. and EMI BLACKWOOD MUSIC INC.
All Rights Reserved International Copyright Secured Used by Permission

Heaven Help Us All

Registration 2
Rhythm: Rock

Words and Music by
Ronald Miller

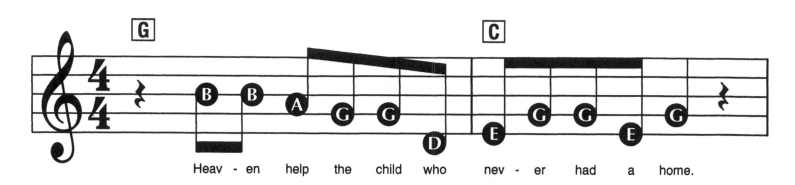

Heav - en help the child who nev - er had a home.

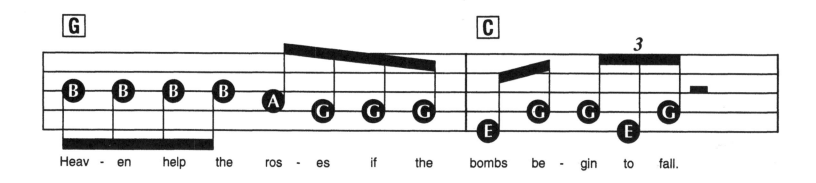

Heav - en help the girl who walks the streets a - lone.

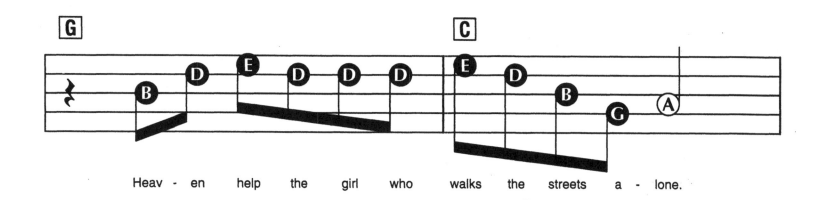

Heav - en help the ros - es if the bombs be - gin to fall.

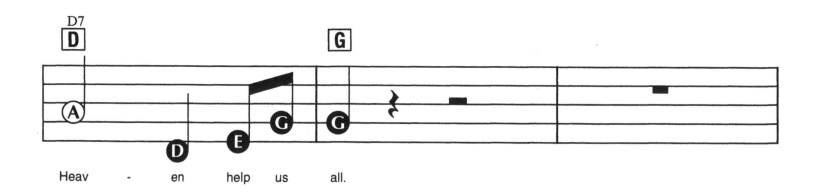

Heav - en help us all.

© 1970, 1973 (Renewed 1998, 2001) STONE DIAMOND MUSIC CORP.
All Rights Controlled and Administered by EMI BLACKWOOD MUSIC INC.
All Rights Reserved   International Copyright Secured   Used by Permission

17

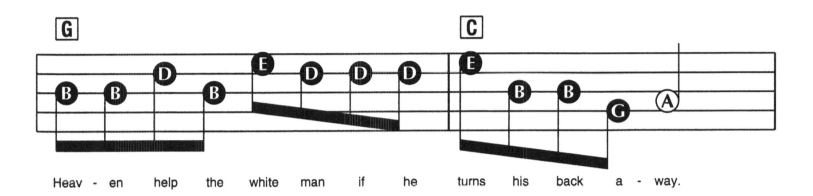

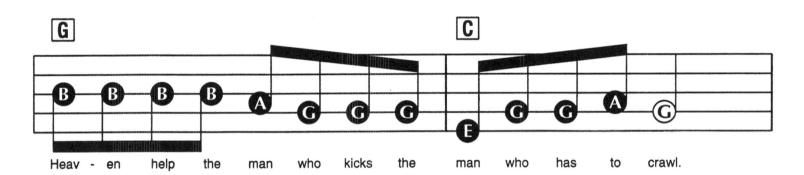

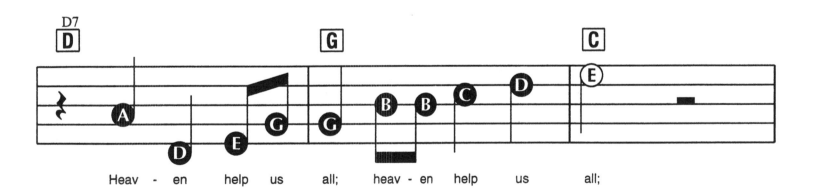

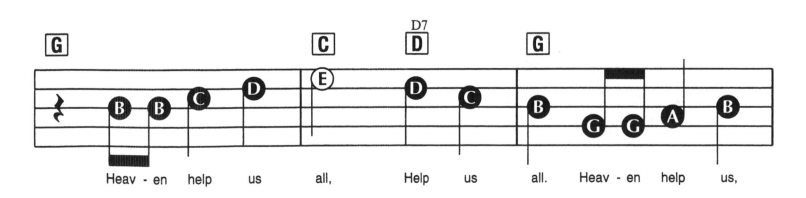

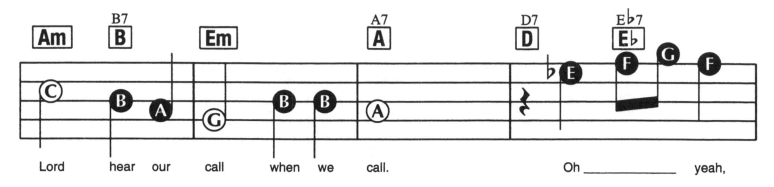

Lord hear our call when we call. Oh _____ yeah,

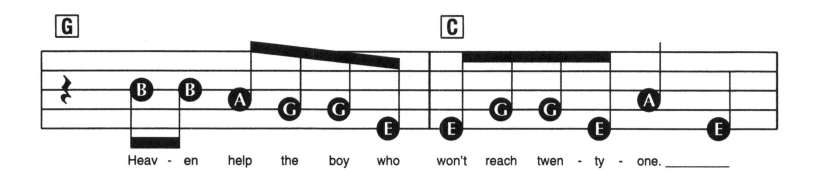

Heav - en help the boy who won't reach twen - ty - one. _____

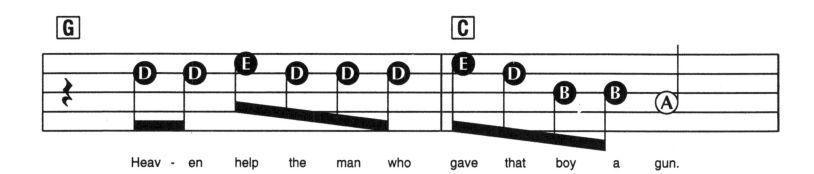

Heav - en help the man who gave that boy a gun.

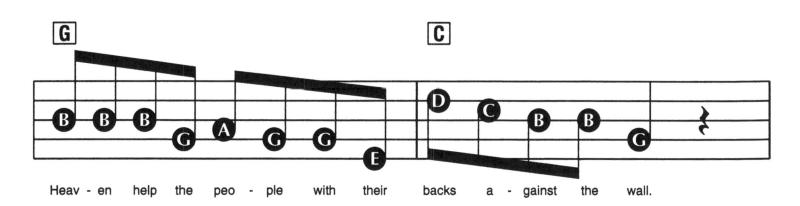

Heav - en help the peo - ple with their backs a - gainst the wall.

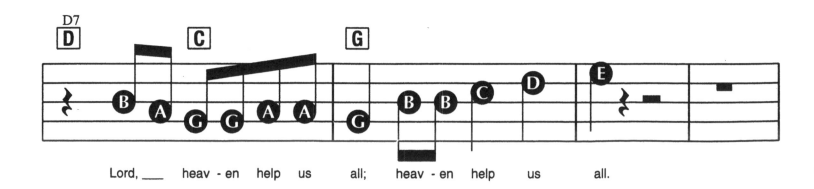

Lord, ___ heav - en help us all; heav - en help us all.

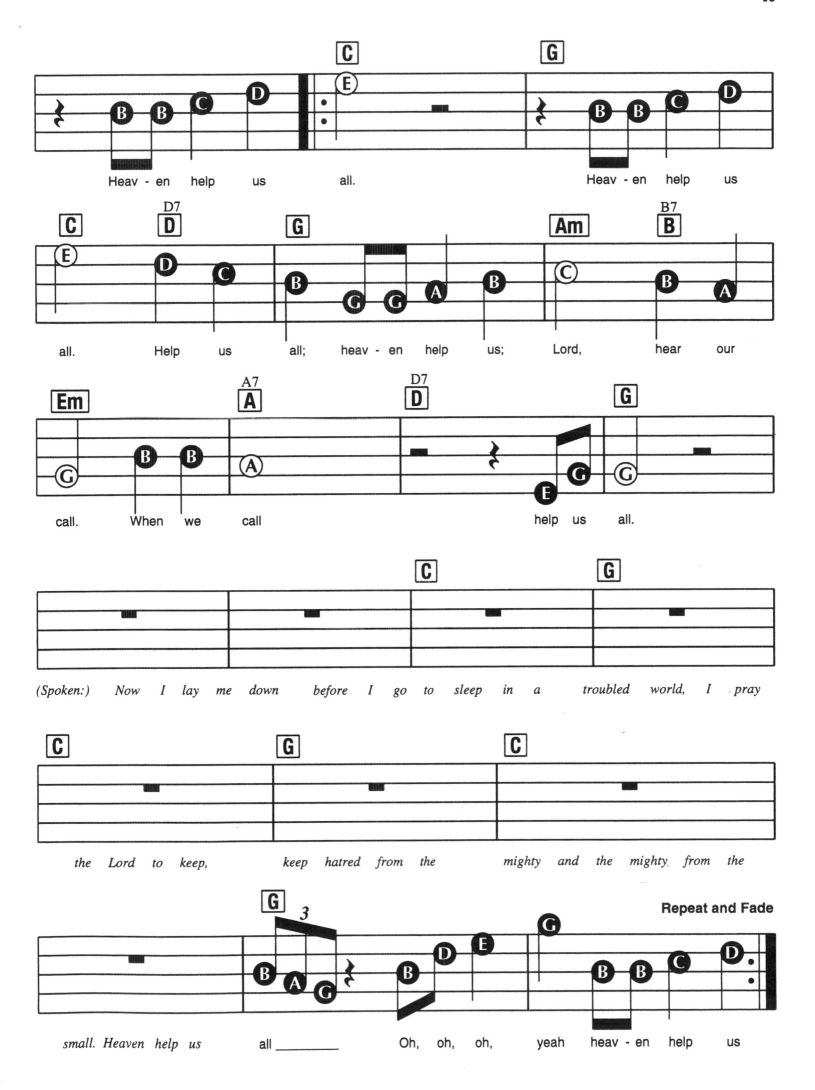

I Just Called to Say I Love You

Registration 2
Rhythm: Rock

Words and Music by
Stevie Wonder

© 1984 JOBETE MUSIC CO., INC. and BLACK BULL MUSIC
c/o EMI APRIL MUSIC INC.
All Rights Reserved   International Copyright Secured   Used by Permission

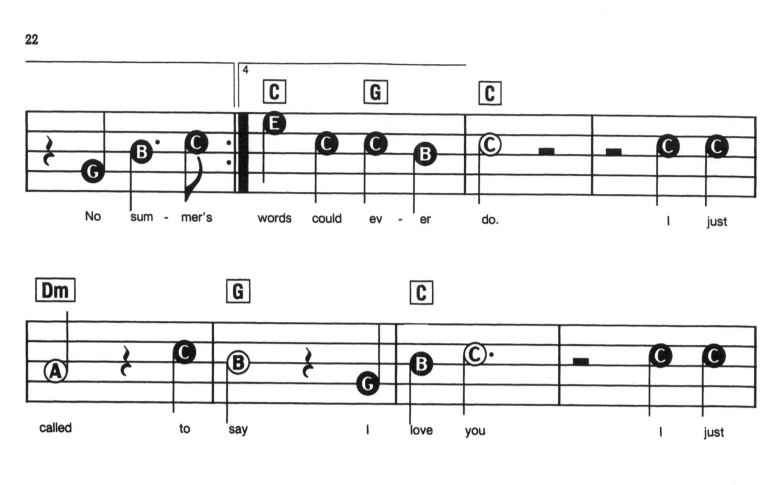

No sum - mer's words could ev - er do. I just

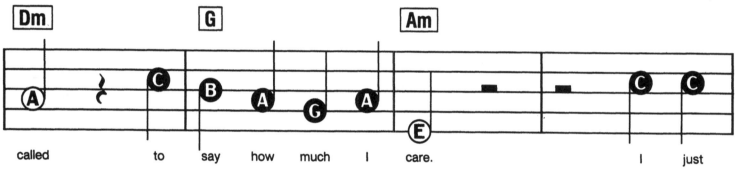

called to say I love you I just

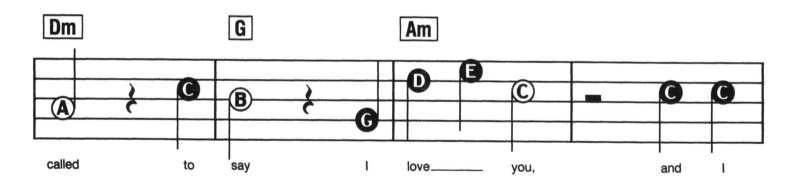

called to say how much I care. I just

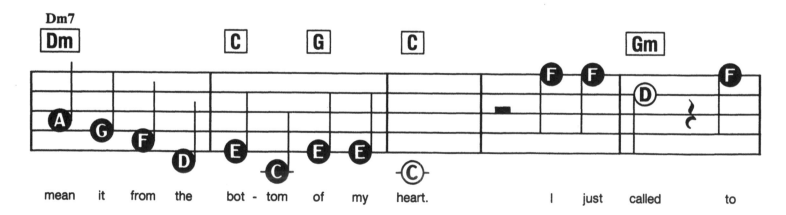

called to say I love_____ you, and I

mean it from the bot - tom of my heart. I just called to

23

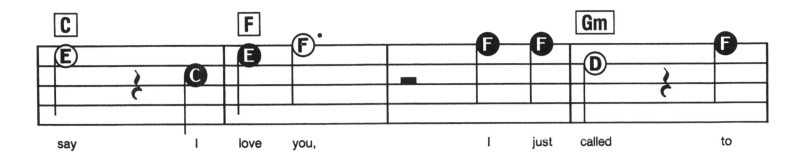

say | love you, | just called to

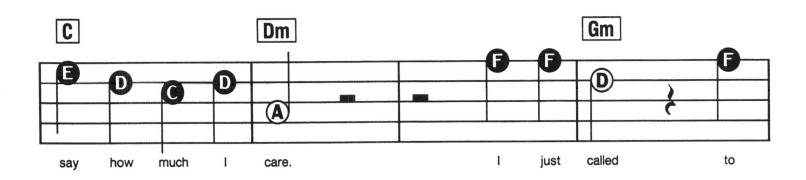

say how much I care. | just called to

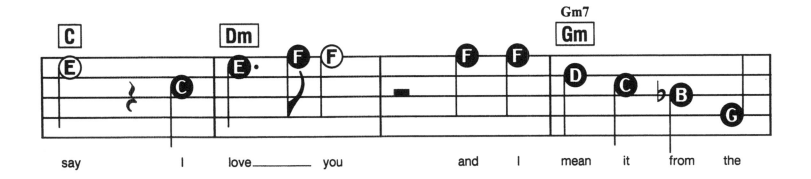

say I love_____ you and I mean it from the

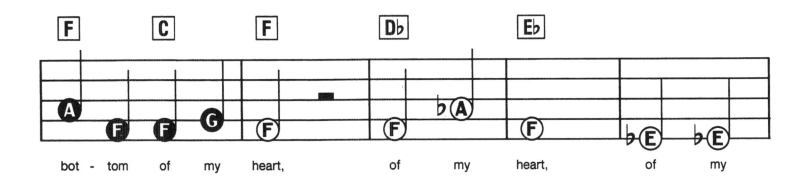

bot - tom of my heart, of my heart, of my

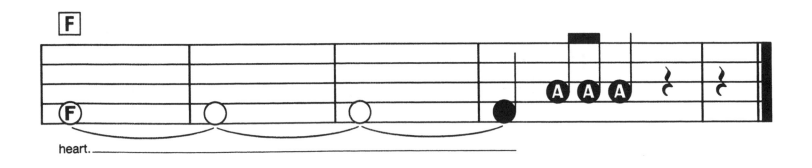

heart._____

I Wish

Registration 9
Rhythm: Rock

Words and Music by
Stevie Wonder

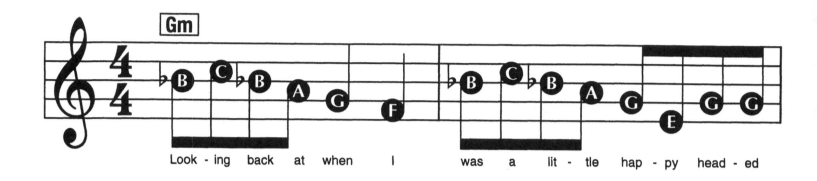

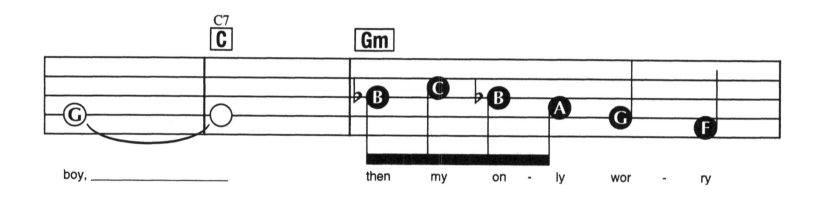

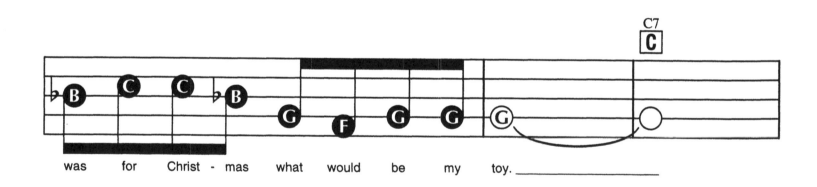

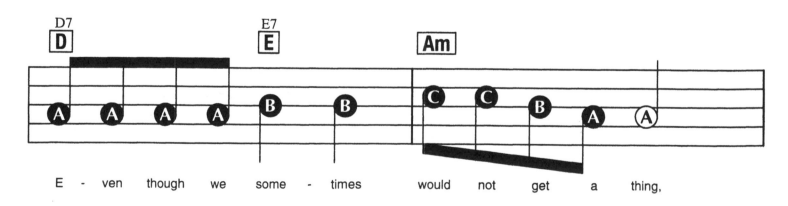

© 1976 JOBETE MUSIC CO., INC. and BLACK BULL MUSIC
c/o EMI APRIL MUSIC INC.
All Rights Reserved   International Copyright Secured   Used by Permission

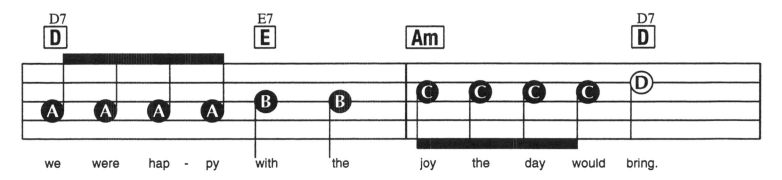

we were hap - py with the joy the day would bring.

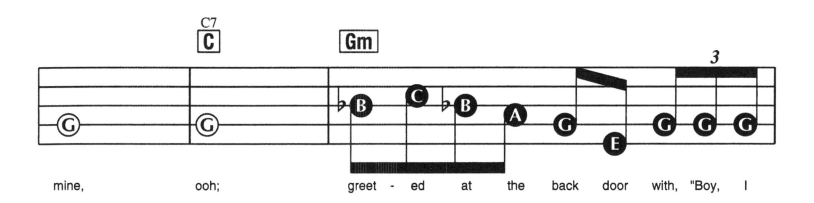

Sneak - in' out the back door to hang out with those hood - lum friends of

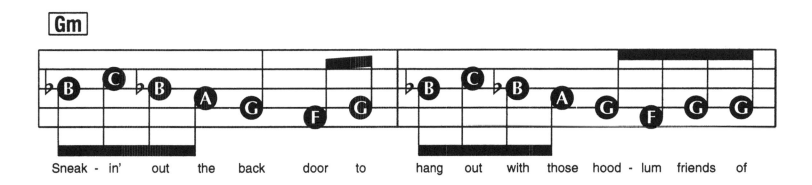

mine, ooh; greet - ed at the back door with, "Boy, I

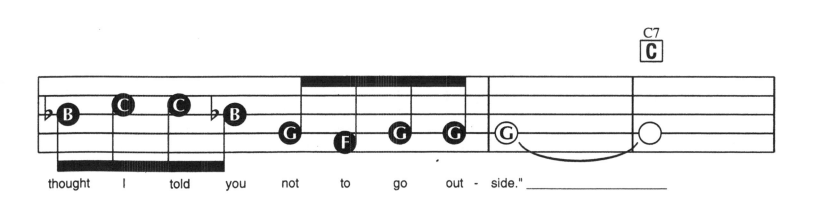

thought I told you not to go out - side." _____

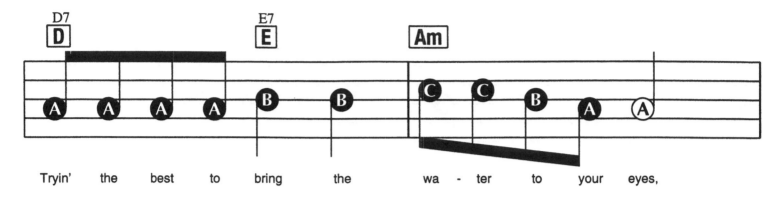

Tryin' the best to bring the wa - ter to your eyes,

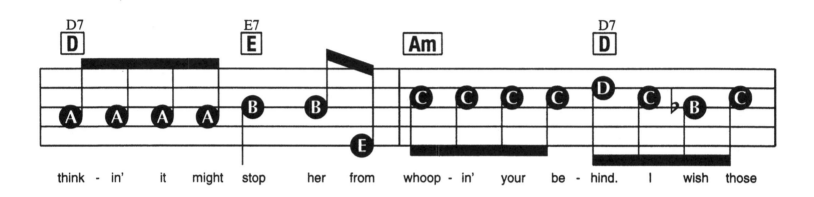

think - in' it might stop her from whoop - in' your be - hind. I wish those

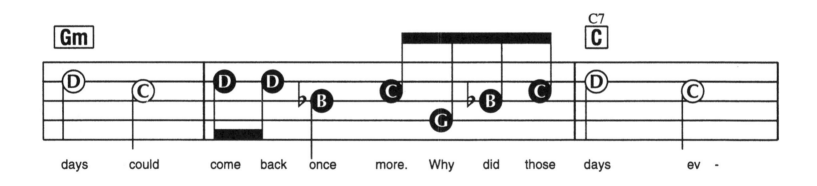

days could come back once more. Why did those days ev -

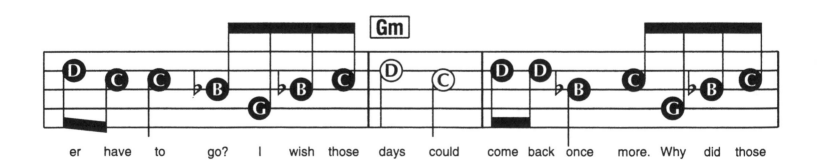

er have to go? I wish those days could come back once more. Why did those

27

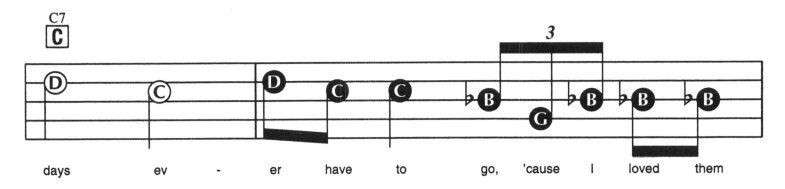

days   ev - er   have   to   go,   'cause   I   loved   them

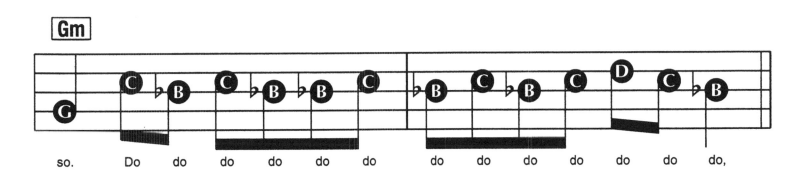

so.   Do   do   do   do   do   do   do   do   do   do   do   do   do,

Repeat and Fade

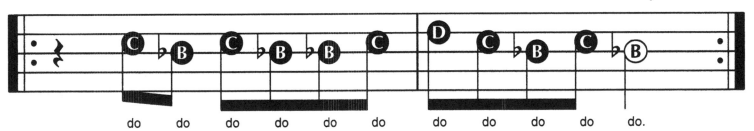

do   do   do   do   do   do   do   do   do   do   do.

Additional Lyrics

Brother says he's tellin'
'Bout you playin' doctor with that girl
Just don't tell, I'll give you
Anything you want in this whole wide world.
Mama gives you money for Sunday school;
You trade yours for candy after church is through.

Smokin' cigarettes and writing something nasty on the wall (you nasty boy);
Teacher sends you to the principal's office down the hall.
You grow up and learn that kinda thing ain't right,
But while you were doin' it - it sure felt outta sight.

I wish those days could come back once more.
Why did those days ever have to go?
I wish those days could come back once more.
Why did those days ever have to go?

If You Really Love Me

Words and Music by
Stevie Wonder and
Syreeta Wright

Registration 8
Rhythm: Rock

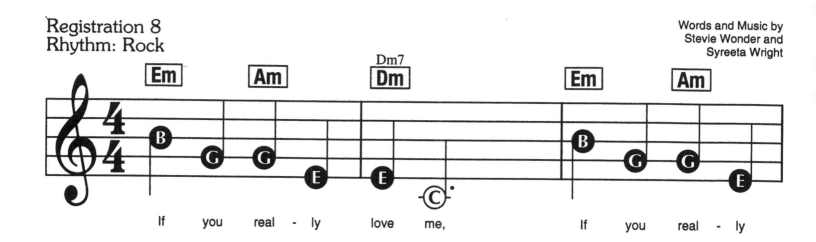

If you real - ly love me, If you real - ly

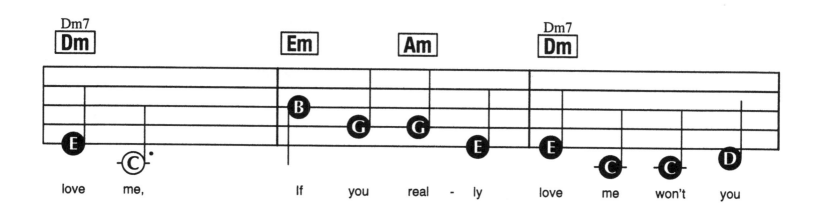

love me, If you real - ly love me won't you

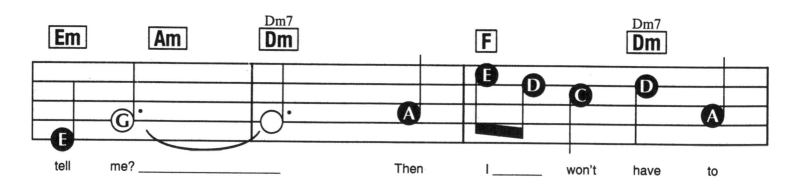

tell me? _____ Then I _____ won't have to

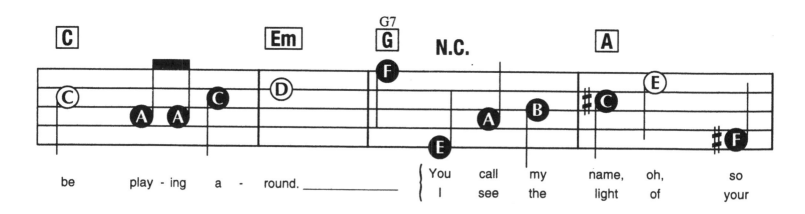

be play - ing a - round. _____ You call my name, oh, so
I see the light of your

© 1970 (Renewed 1998) JOBETE MUSIC CO., INC. and BLACK BULL MUSIC
c/o EMI APRIL MUSIC INC.
All Rights Reserved   International Copyright Secured   Used by Permission

29

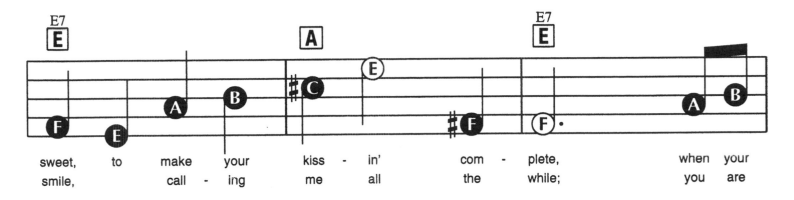

sweet, to make your kiss - in' com - plete, when your
smile, call - ing me all the while; you are

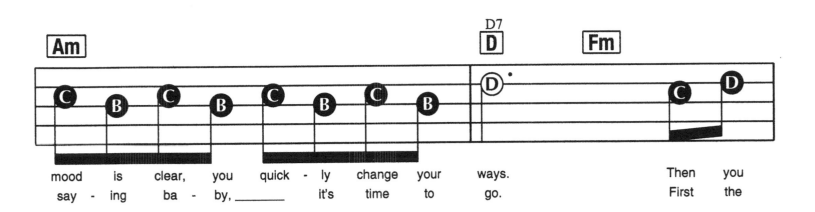

mood is clear, you quick - ly change your ways. Then you
say - ing ba - by, _____ it's time to go. First the

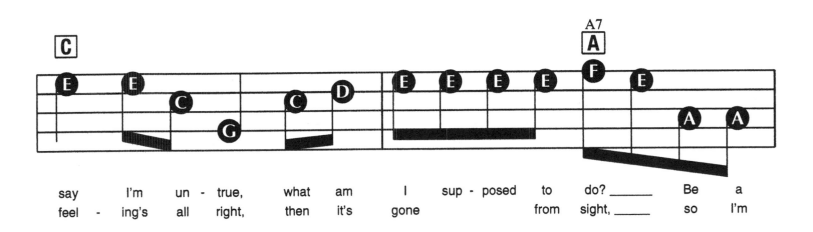

say I'm un - true, what am I sup - posed to do? _____ Be a
feel - ing's all right, then it's gone from sight, _____ so I'm

Last time
Repeat and Fade

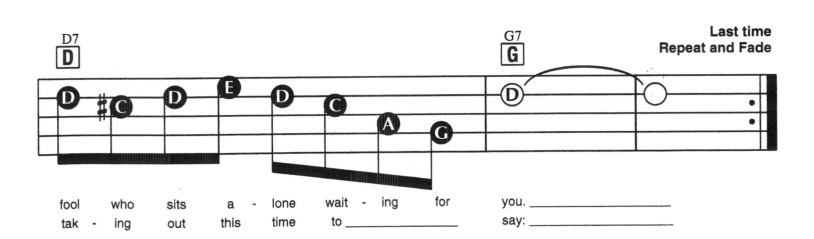

fool who sits a - lone wait - ing for you. _____
tak - ing out this time to _____ say: _____

Higher Ground

Registration 4
Rhythm: Rock or Disco

Words and Music by
Stevie Wonder

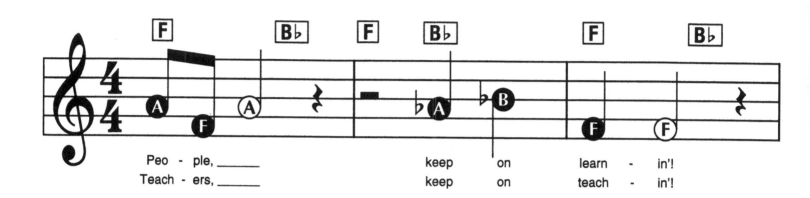

Peo - ple, _____ keep on learn - in'!
Teach - ers, _____ keep on teach - in'!

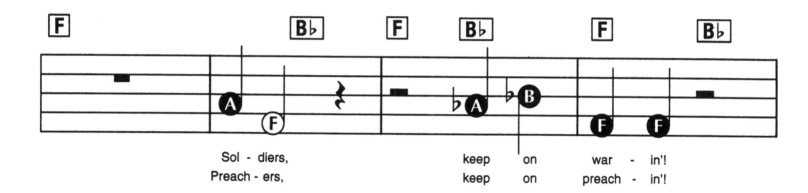

Sol - diers, keep on war - in'!
Preach - ers, keep on preach - in'!

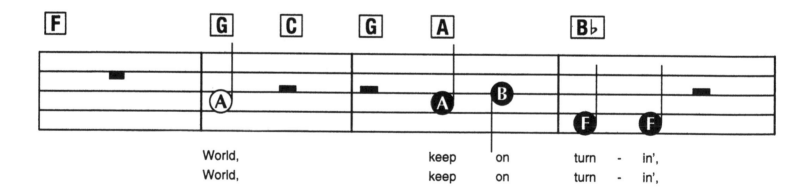

World, keep on turn - in',
World, keep on turn - in',

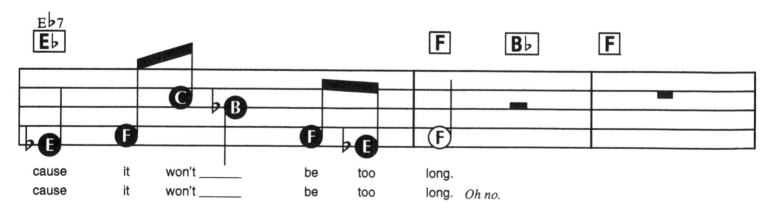

cause it won't _____ be too long.
cause it won't _____ be too long. *Oh no.*

© 1973 (Renewed 2001) JOBETE MUSIC CO., INC. and BLACK BULL MUSIC
c/o EMI APRIL MUSIC INC.
All Rights Reserved   International Copyright Secured   Used by Permission

Additional Lyrics

4. Don't you let nobody bring you down. They'll sho' nuff try.
God is gonna show you Higher Ground. He's the only friend you have around.

Living for the City

Registration 9
Rhythm: Rock

Words and Music by
Stevie Wonder

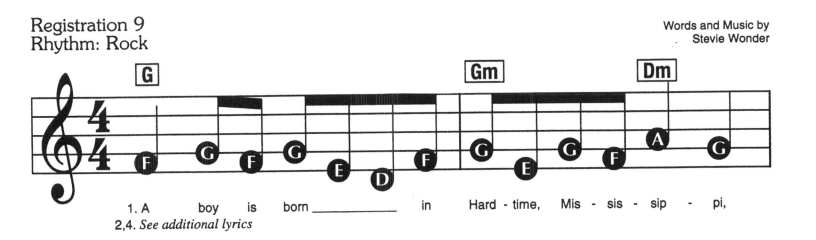

1. A boy is born _____ in Hard - time, Mis - sis - sip - pi,
2,4. *See additional lyrics*

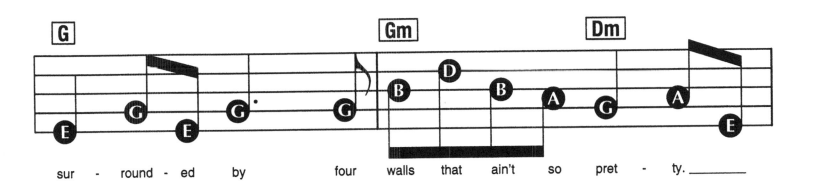

sur - round - ed by four walls that ain't so pret - ty. _____

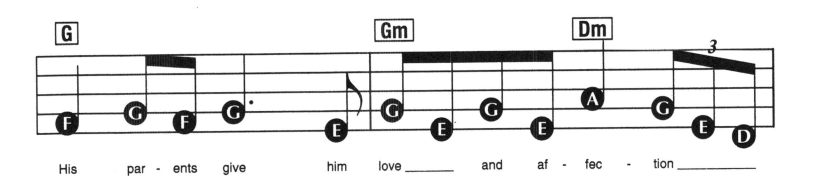

His par - ents give him love _____ and af - fec - tion _____

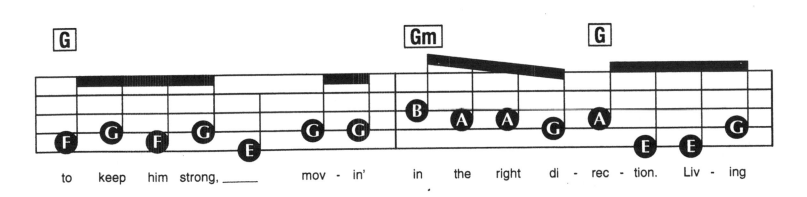

to keep him strong, _____ mov - in' in the right di - rec - tion. Liv - ing

© 1973 (Renewed 2001) JOBETE MUSIC CO., INC. and BLACK BULL MUSIC
c/o EMI APRIL MUSIC INC.
All Rights Reserved   International Copyright Secured   Used by Permission

34

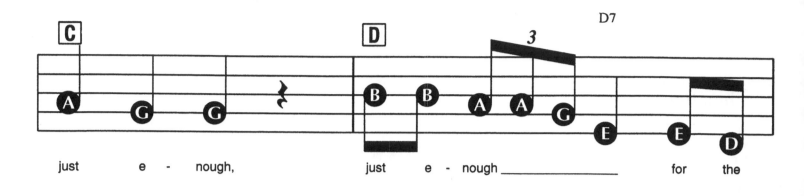

just e - nough,   just e - nough _____ for the

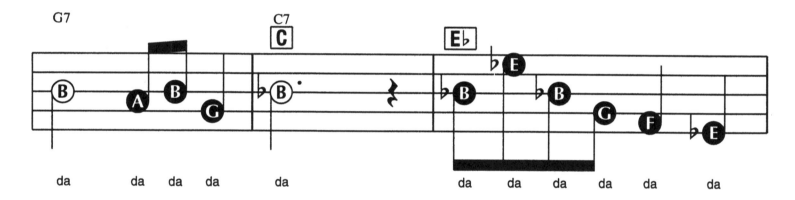

ci - ty.   Yeah,   Da da da

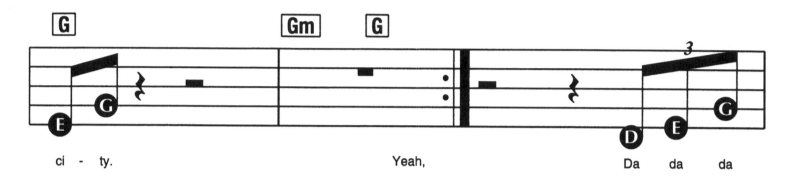

da   da da da   da   da   da   da   da   da   da

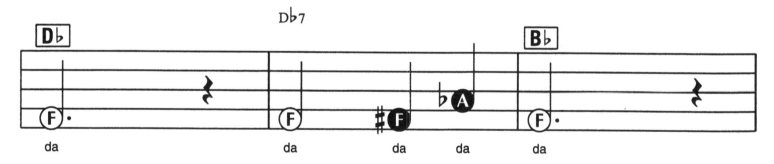

da   da   da   da   da

D.C. al Coda
(Return to beginning,
Play to ✦ and
Skip to Coda)

To Coda ✦

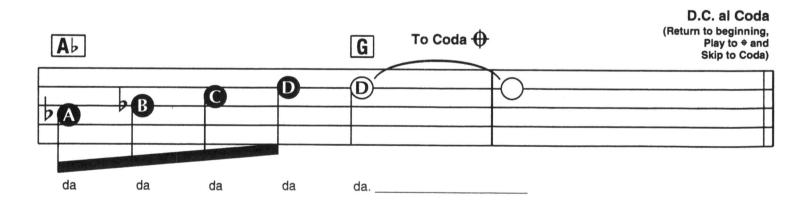

da   da   da   da   da. _____

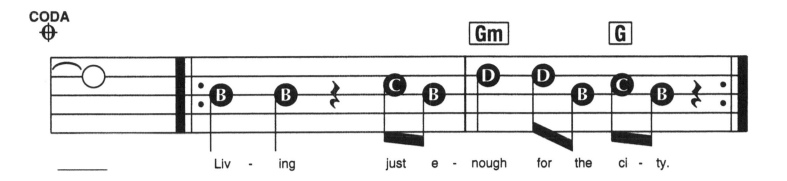

Liv - ing   just e - nough   for   the   ci - ty.

Additional Lyrics

2. His father works some days for fourteen hours,
   And you can bet he barely makes a dollar.
   His mother goes to scrub the follrs for many,
   And you'd best believe she hardly gets a penny.
   Living just enough, just enough for the city.

3. His sister's black, but she is sho'nuff pretty.
   Her skirt is short, but Lord her legs are sturdy.
   To walk to school, she's got to get up early.
   Her clothes are old, but never are they dirty.
   Living just enough, just enough for the city.

4. Her brother's smart, he's got more sense than many.
   His patience's long, but soon he won't have any.
   To find a job is like a haaystack needle, 'cause
   Where he lives, they don't use colored people.
   Living just enough, just enough for the city.

Love Light in Flight

Registration 6
Rhythm: Rock

Words and Music by
Stevie Wonder

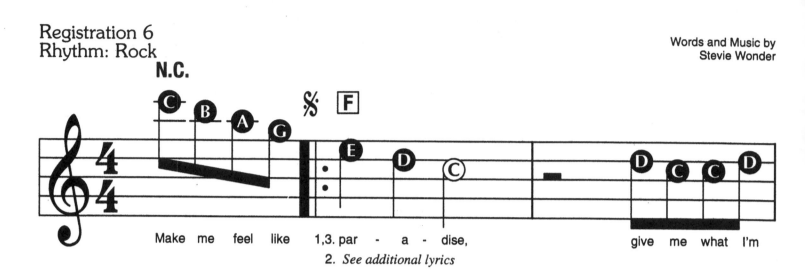

Make me feel like 1,3. par - a - dise,
2. *See additional lyrics*
give me what I'm

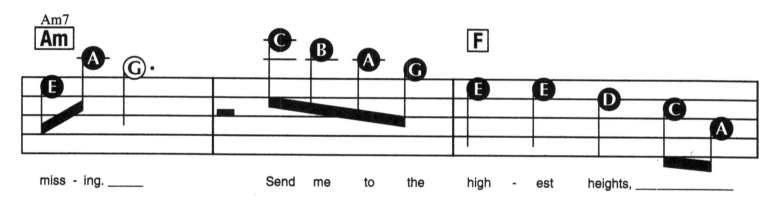

miss - ing. _____ Send me to the high - est heights, _____

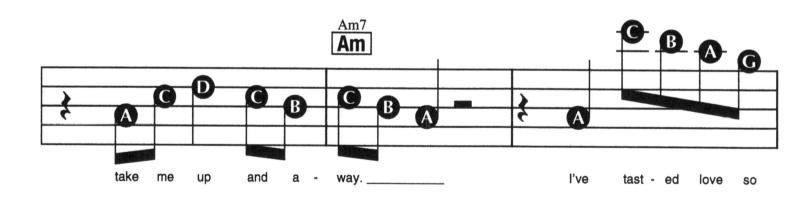

take me up and a - way. _____ I've tast - ed love so

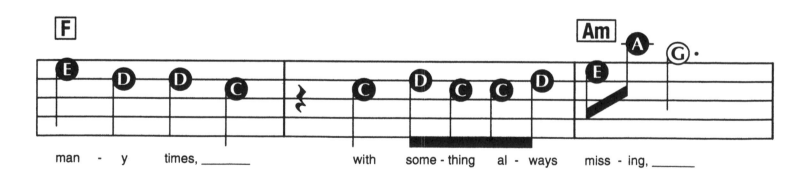

man - y times, _____ with some - thing al - ways miss - ing, _____

© 1984 JOBETE MUSIC CO., INC. and BLACK BULL MUSIC
c/o EMI APRIL MUSIC INC.
All Rights Reserved International Copyright Secured Used by Permission

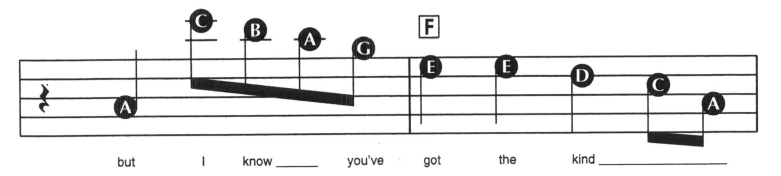

but   I   know   you've   got   the   kind

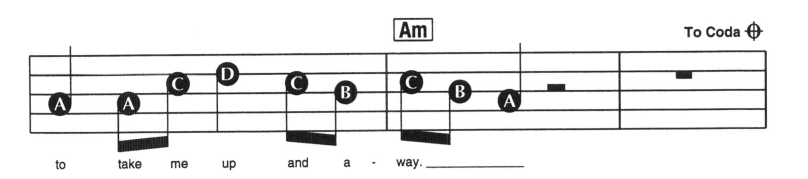

to   take   me   up   and   a -   way.

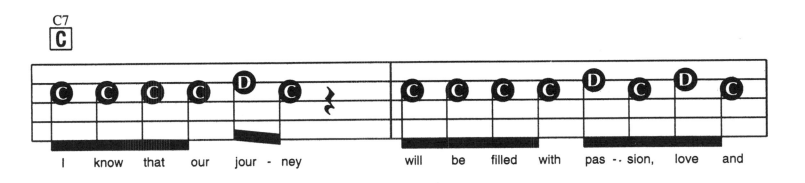

I   know   that   our   jour - ney   will   be   filled   with   pas -- sion,   love   and

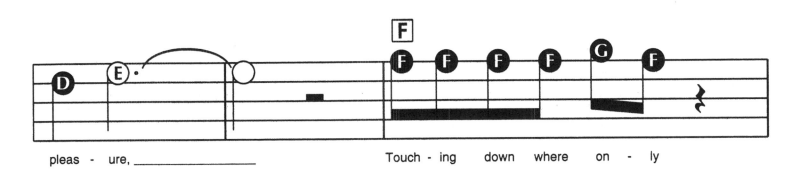

pleas - ure,   Touch - ing   down   where   on - ly

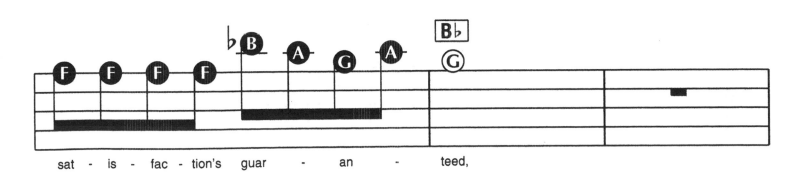

sat - is - fac - tion's   guar - an - teed,

38

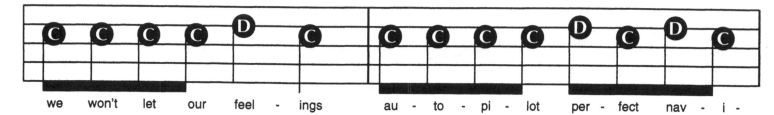

we won't let our feel - ings au - to - pi - lot per - fect nav - i -

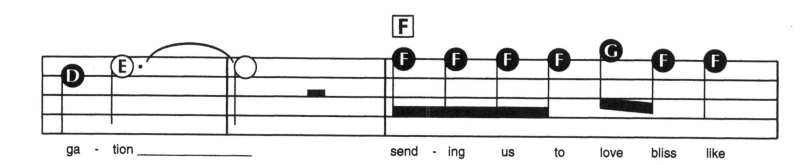

ga - tion _____ send - ing us to love bliss like

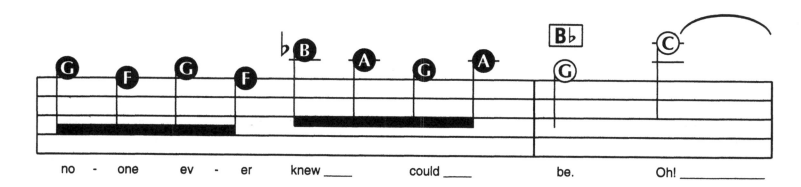

no - one ev - er knew ____ could ____ be. Oh! _____

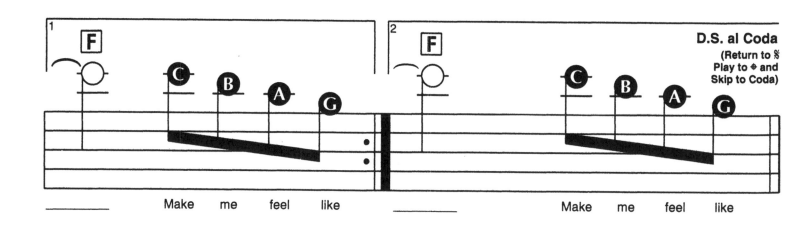

Make me feel like _____ Make me feel like

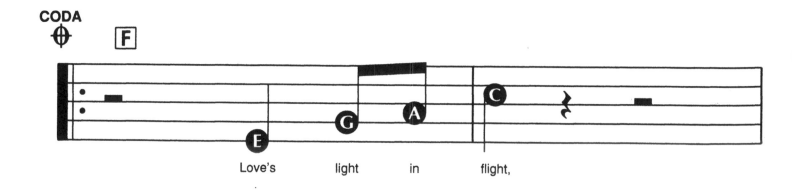

CODA

Love's light in flight,

fuel   in - jec - tion   pas - sion!   Love's   light   in

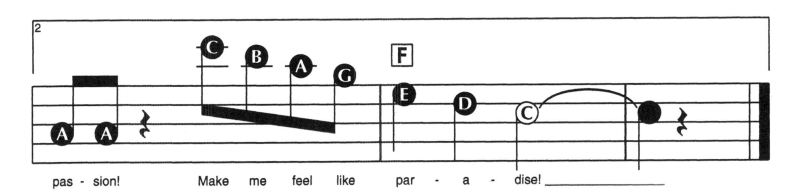

flight, _____   fuel   in - jec - tion   pas - sion!

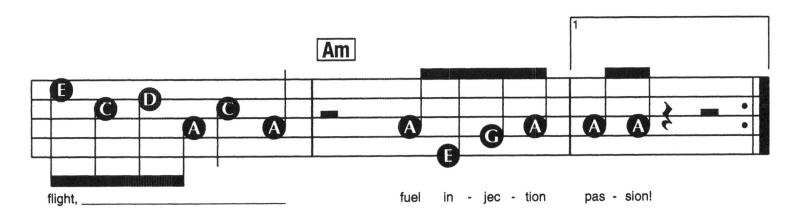

pas - sion!   Make   me   feel   like   par - a - dise! _____

Additional Lyrics

2. Make me feel like paradise, fill me with your kisses.
Make the moment feel just right, take me up and away.
'Cause I have waited all my life, for the one worth giving,
And I don't have to think it twice, let's go up and away!

We need just to feel it to know that our lovin' has the power,
Showing that these feelings emanate from you and me.
With love high aviation, we will fly forever and one hour,
Giving us the always to live out all our fantasies.

My Cherie Amour

Registration 7
Rhythm: Rock or Bossa Nova

Words and Music by Stevie Wonder,
Sylvia Moy and Henry Cosby

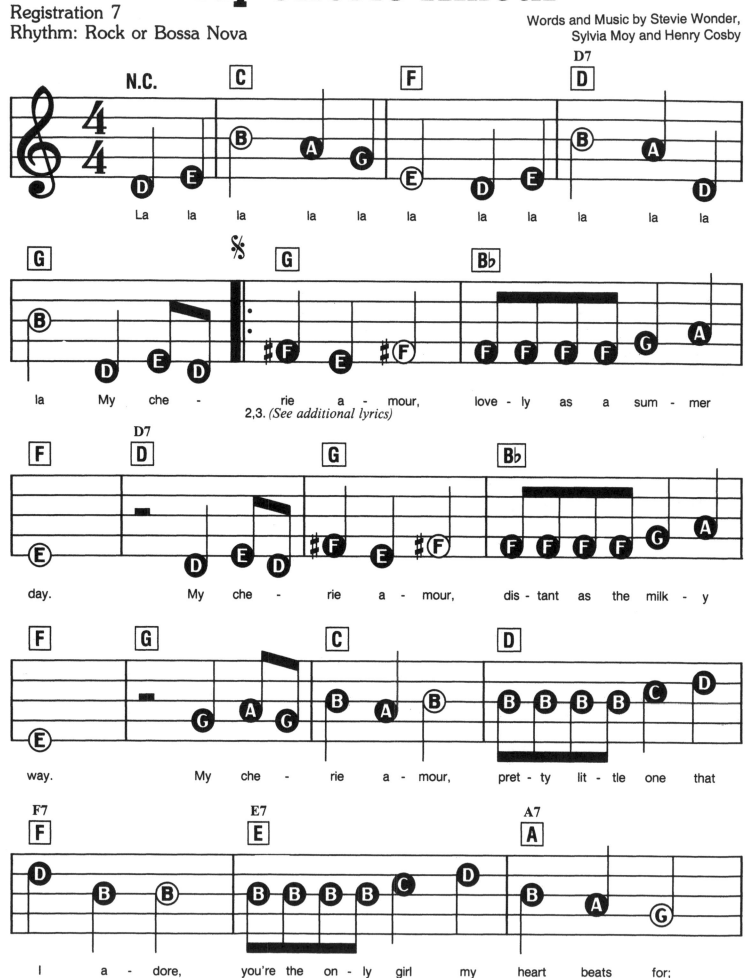

© 1968 (Renewed 1996) JOBETE MUSIC CO., INC., BLACK BULL MUSIC and SAWANDI MUSIC
c/o EMI APRIL MUSIC INC. and EMI BLACKWOOD MUSIC INC.
All Rights Reserved   International Copyright Secured   Used by Permission

41

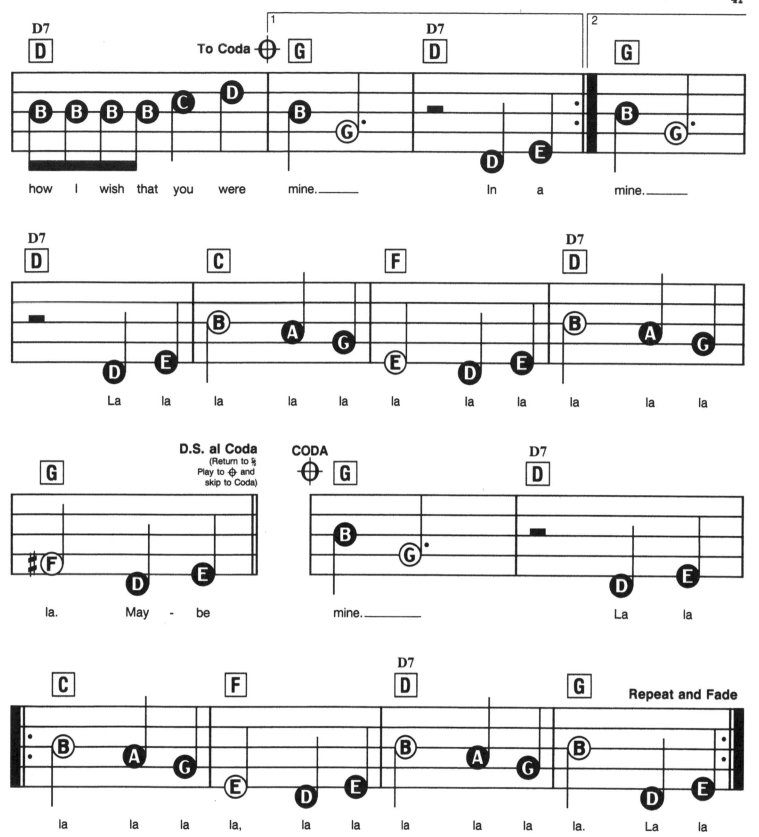

Additional Lyrics

2. In a cafe, or sometimes on a crowded street,
   I've been near you, but you never notice me.
   My cherie amour, won't you tell me how could you ignore,
   That behind that little smile I wore, how I wish that you were mine.

3. Maybe someday you'll see my face among the crowd;
   Maybe someday I'll share your little distant cloud.
   Oh, cherie amour, pretty little one that I adore,
   You're the only girl my heart beats for; how I wish that you were mine.

Overjoyed

Registration 7
Rhythm: Ballad or Rock

Words and Music by
Stevie Wonder

© 1985 JOBETE MUSIC CO., INC. and BLACK BULL MUSIC
c/o EMI APRIL MUSIC INC.
All Rights Reserved   International Copyright Secured   Used by Permission

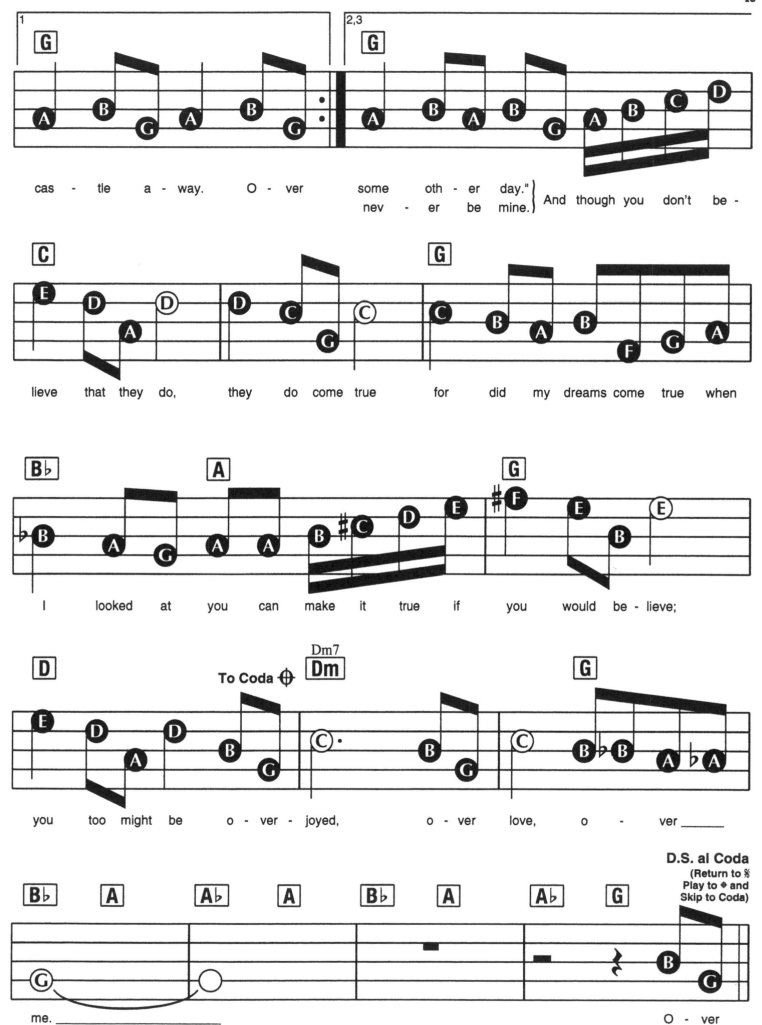

44

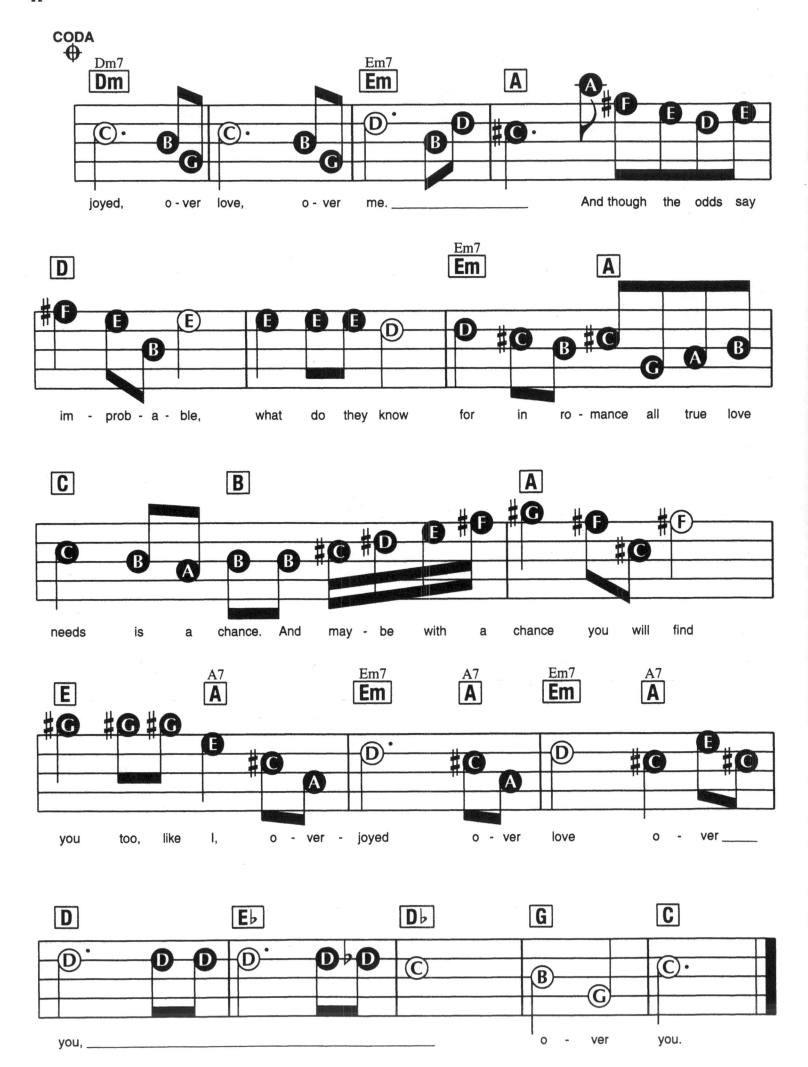

Part Time Lover

Registration 6
Rhythm: Disco

Words and Music by
Stevie Wonder

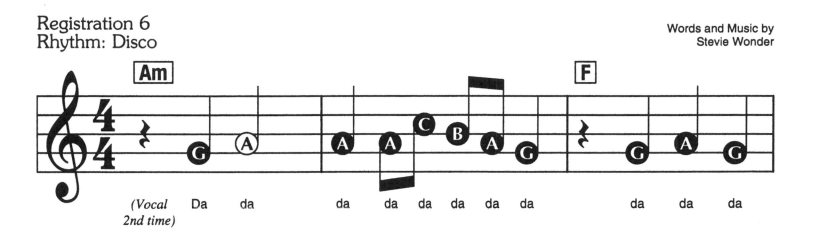

*(Vocal Da   da   da   da   da   da   da   da   da   da   da
2nd time)*

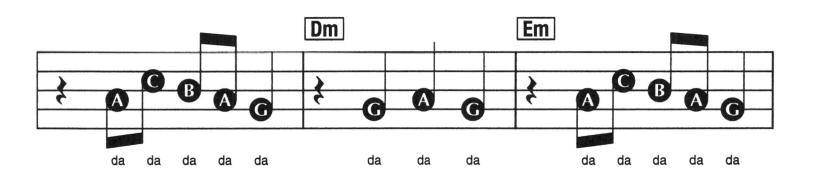

da   da   da   da   da   da   da   da   da   da   da   da   da

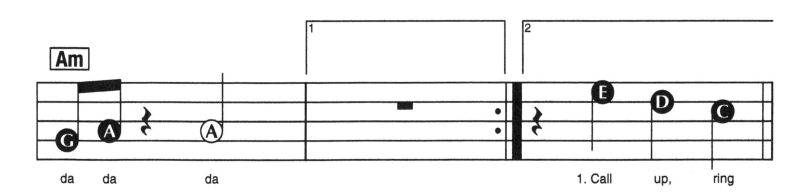

da   da   da   1. Call   up,   ring

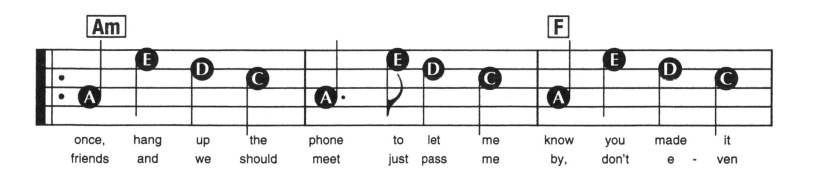

once,   hang   up   the   phone   to   let   me   know   you   made   it
friends   and   we   should   meet   just   pass   me   by,   don't   e - ven

© 1985 JOBETE MUSIC CO., INC. and BLACK BULL MUSIC
c/o EMI APRIL MUSIC INC.
All Rights Reserved   International Copyright Secured   Used by Permission

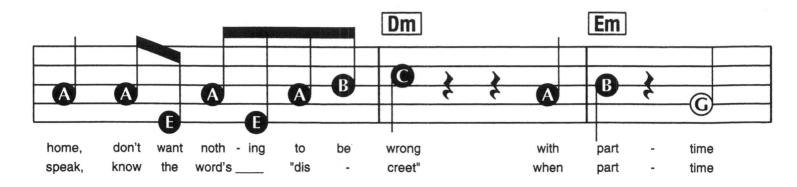

home, don't want noth - ing to be wrong with part - time
speak, know the word's ___ "dis - creet" when part - time

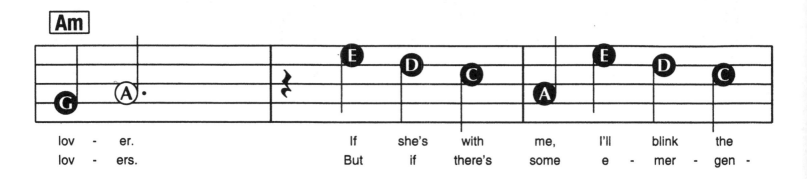

lov - er. If she's with me, I'll blink the
lov - ers. But if there's some e - mer - gen -

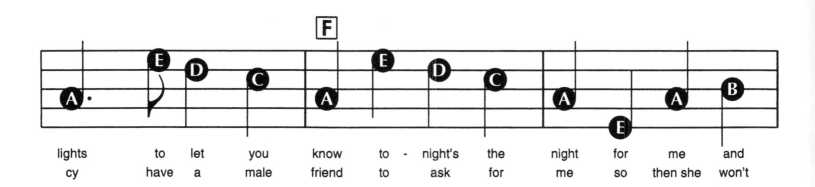

lights to let you know to - night's the night for me and
cy have a male friend to ask for me so then she won't

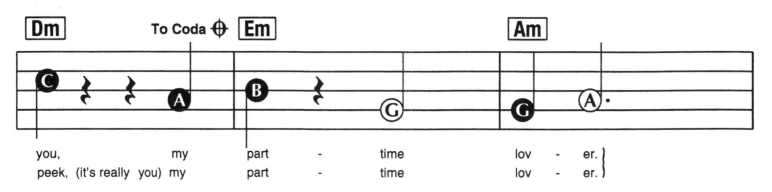

you, my part - time lov - er.
peek, (it's really you) my part - time lov - er.

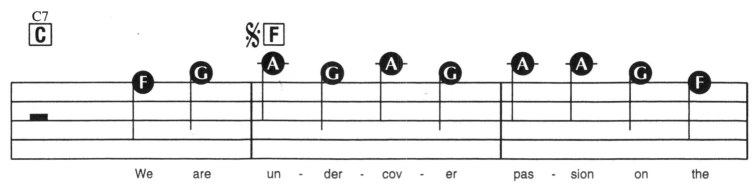

We are un - der - cov - er pas - sion on the

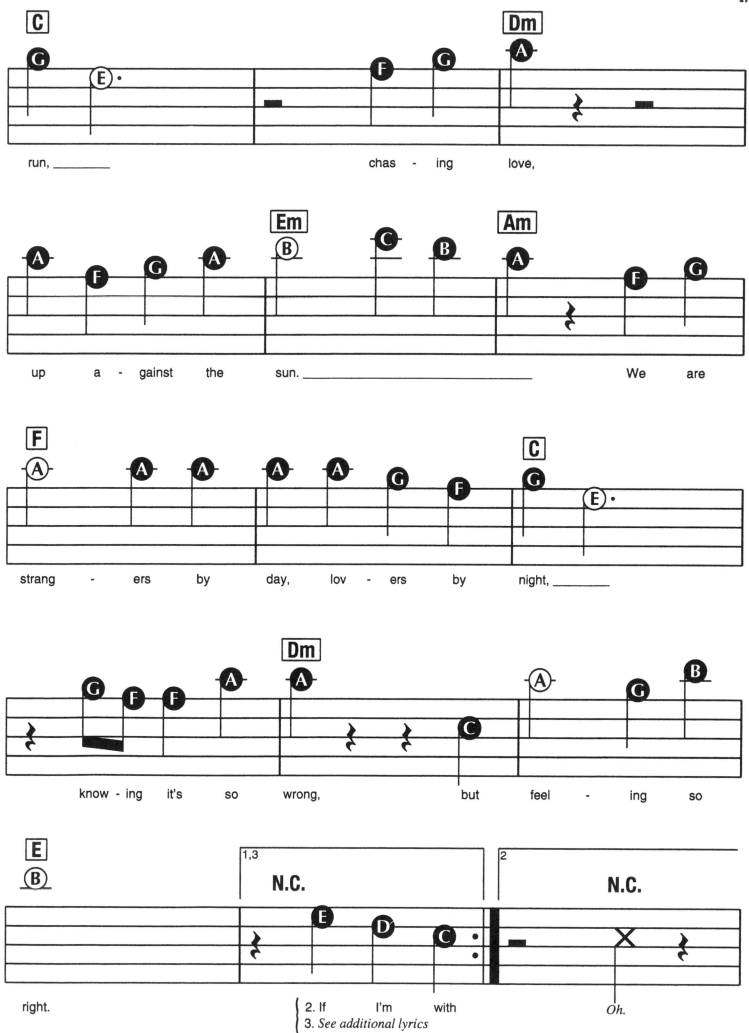

48

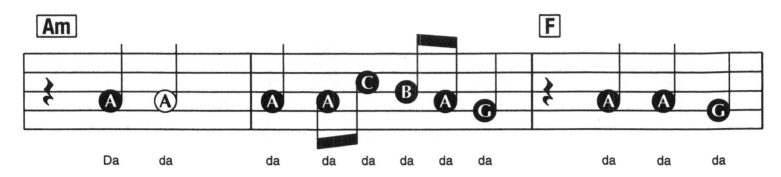

Da da da da da da da da da da da

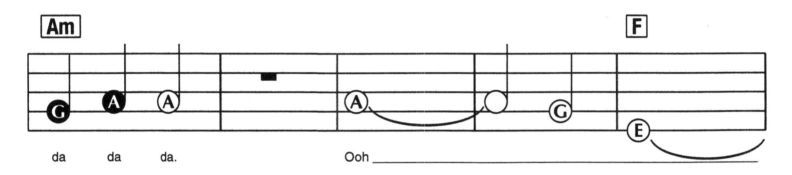

da da da da da da da do do do do ba da da da

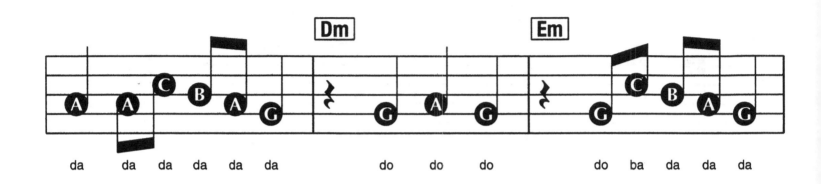

da da da. Ooh

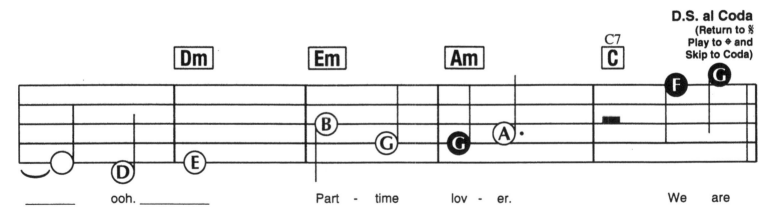

ooh. Part - time lov - er. We are

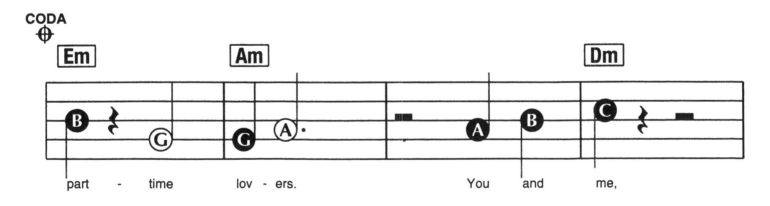

part - time lov - ers. You and me,

49

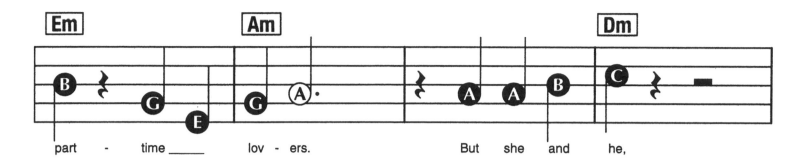

part - time _____ lov - ers. But she and he,

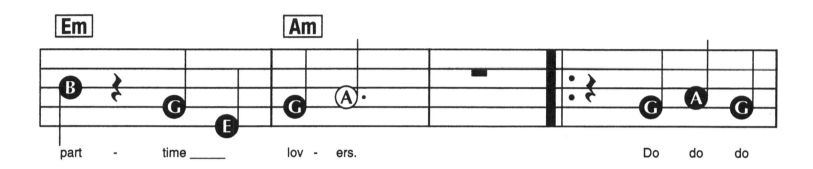

part - time _____ lov - ers. Do do do

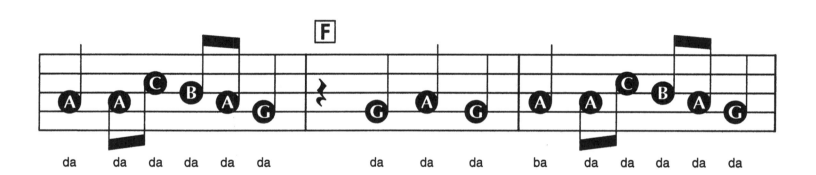

da da da da da da da da da ba da da da da da

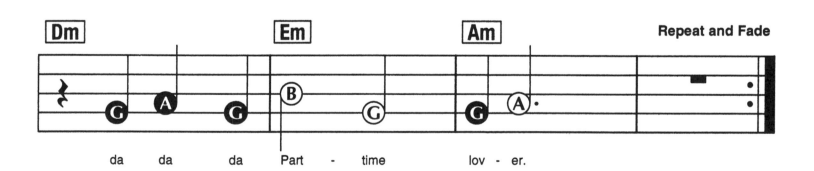

da da da Part - time lov - er.

Additional Lyrics

3. I've got something that I must tell;
Last night someone rang our doorbell
And it was not you, my part- time lover.
And then a man called our exchange
But didn't want to leave his name,
I guess that two can play the game of *(Skip to Coda)*

A Place in the Sun

Registration 8
Rhythm: Rock or Latin

Words and Music by Ronald Miller
and Bryan Wells

© 1966, 1967 (Renewed 1994, 1995) JOBETE MUSIC CO., INC. and STONE DIAMOND MUSIC CORP.
All Rights Controlled and Administered by EMI APRIL MUSIC INC. and EMI BLACKWOOD MUSIC INC.
All Rights Reserved   International Copyright Secured   Used by Permission

51

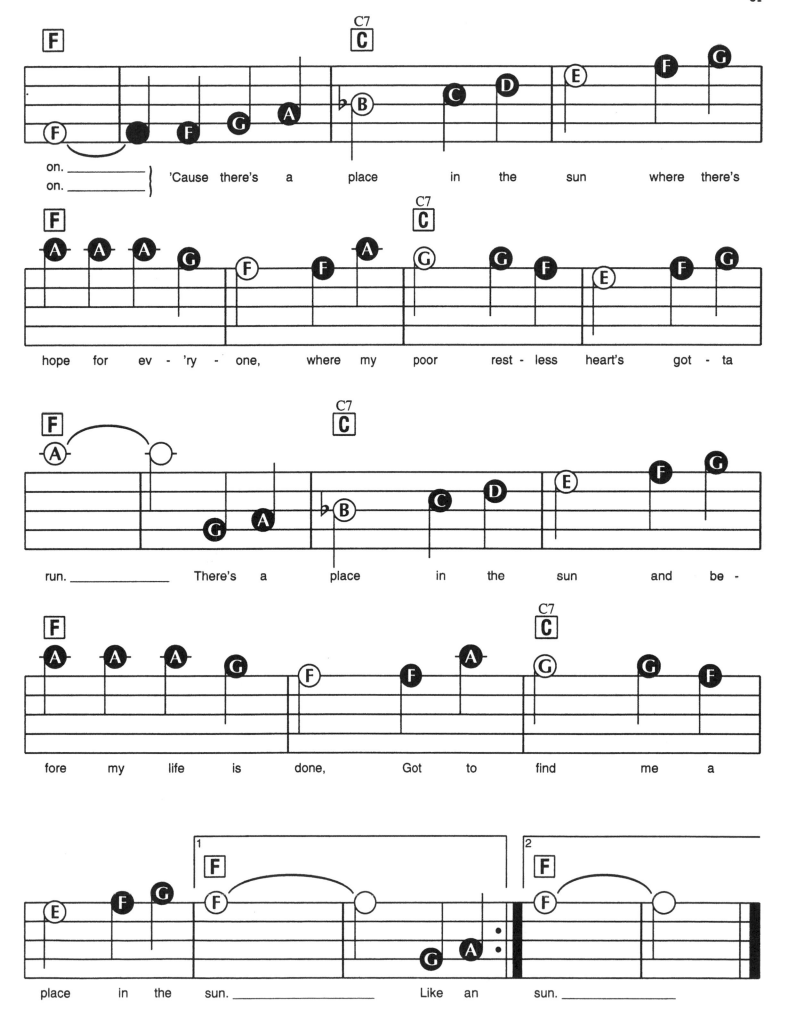

Ribbon in the Sky

Registration 2
Rhythm: Rock

Words and Music by
Stevie Wonder

© 1982 JOBETE MUSIC CO., INC. and BLACK BULL MUSIC
c/o EMI APRIL MUSIC INC.
All Rights Reserved   International Copyright Secured   Used by Permission

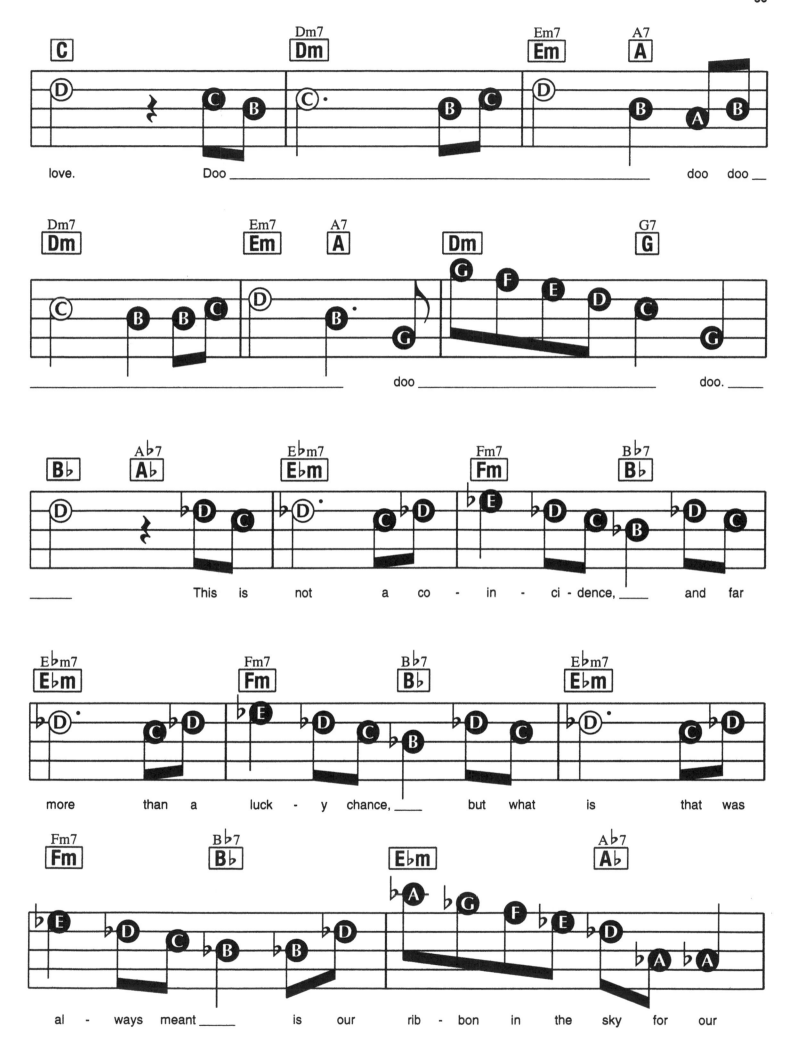

54

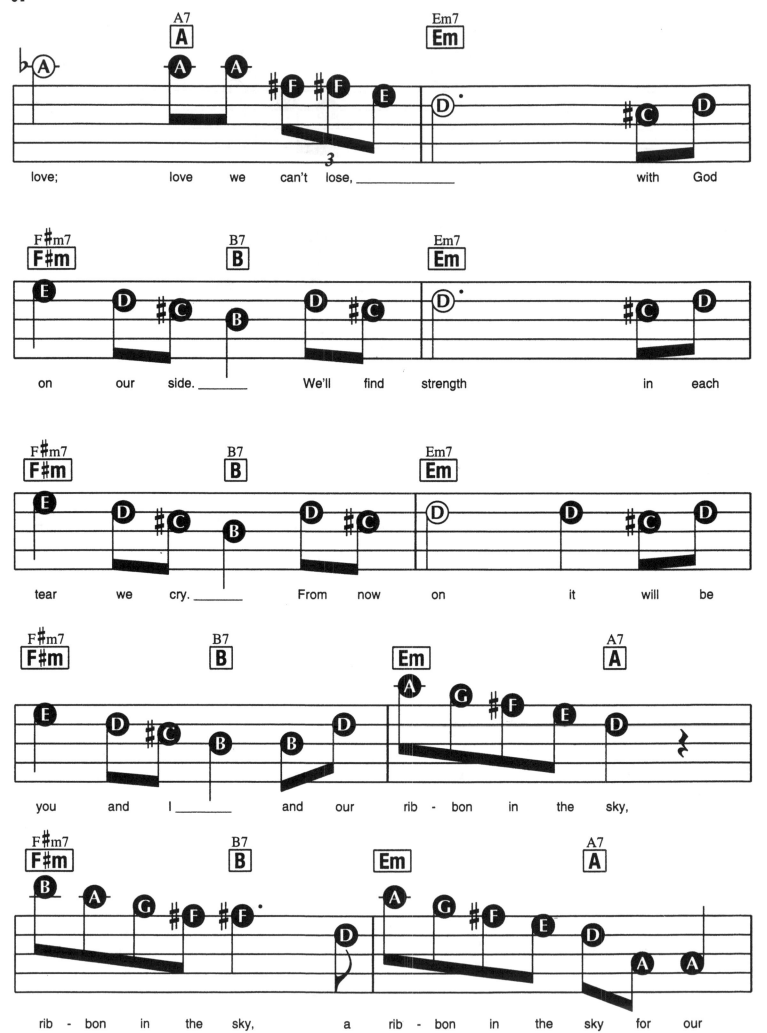

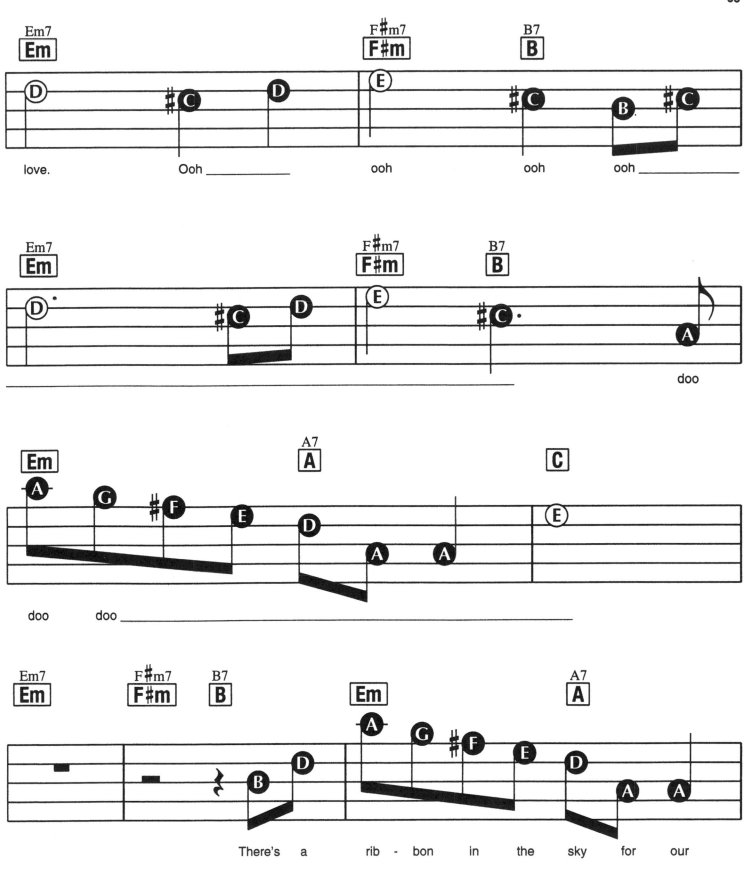

love.　　　　Ooh _____　　ooh　　ooh　　ooh _____

doo

doo　　doo _____

There's　a　rib - bon　in　the　sky　for　our

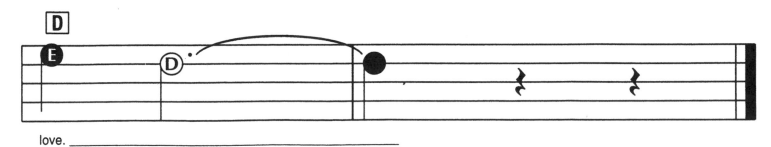

love. _____

Send One Your Love

Registration 3
Rhythm: Rock

Words and Music by
Stevie Wonder

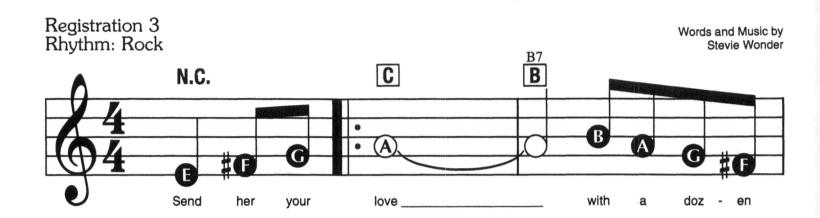

Send her your love — with a doz - en

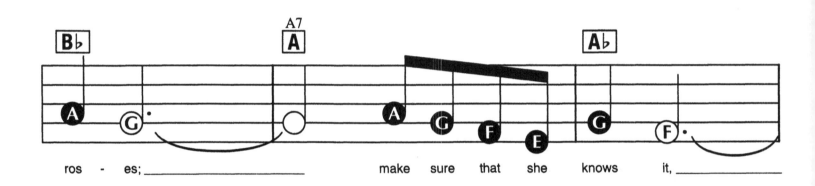

ros - es; — make sure that she knows it, —

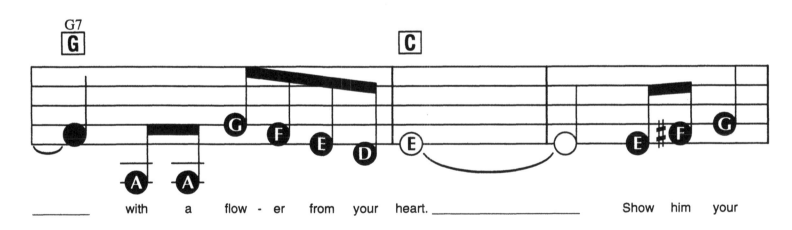

— with a flow - er from your heart. — Show him your

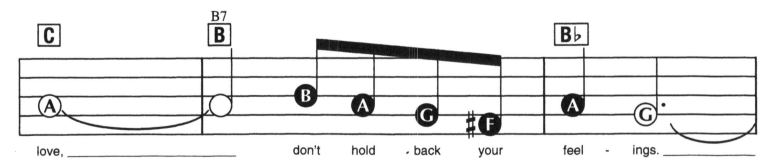

love, — don't hold back your feel - ings. —

© 1979 JOBETE MUSIC CO., INC. and BLACK BULL MUSIC
c/o EMI APRIL MUSIC INC.
All Rights Reserved   International Copyright Secured   Used by Permission

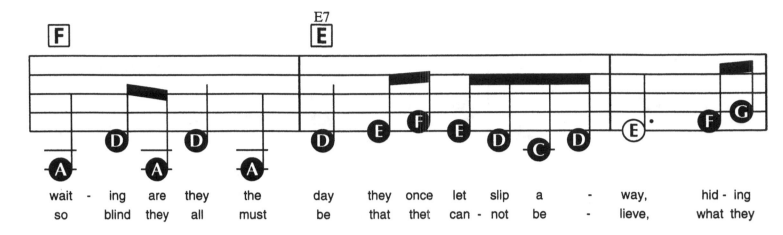

wait - ing are they the day they once let slip a - way, hid - ing
so blind they all must be that thet can - not be - lieve, what they

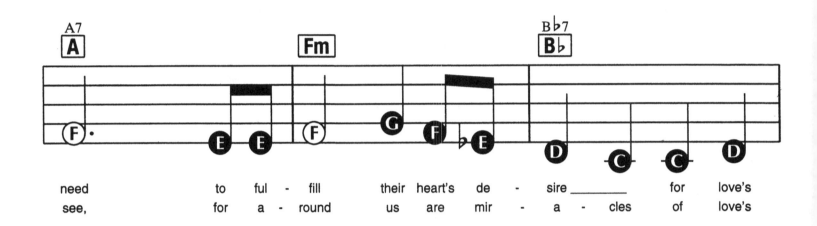

need to ful - fill their heart's de - sire _____ for love's
see, for a - round us are mir - a - cles of love's

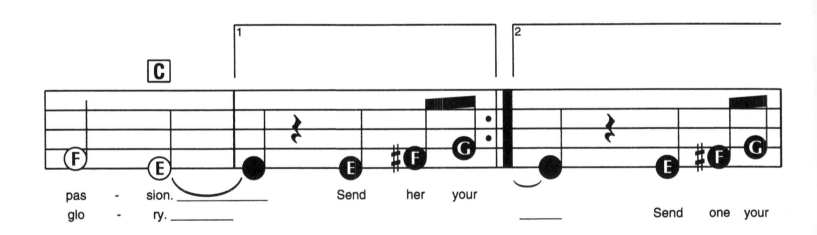

pas - sion. _____ Send her your
glo - ry. _____ _____ Send one your

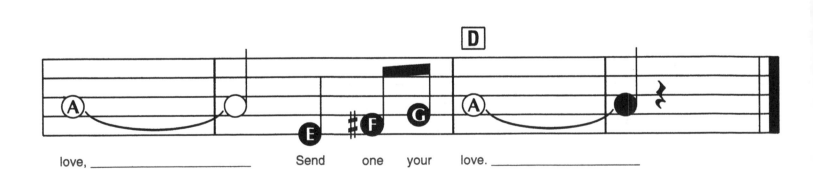

love, _____ Send one your love. _____

Signed, Sealed, Delivered I'm Yours

Registration 7
Rhythm: Rock or 8-Beat

Words and Music by Stevie Wonder, Syreeta Wright,
Lee Garrett and Lula Mae Hardaway

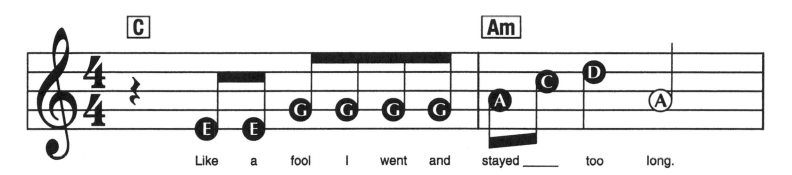

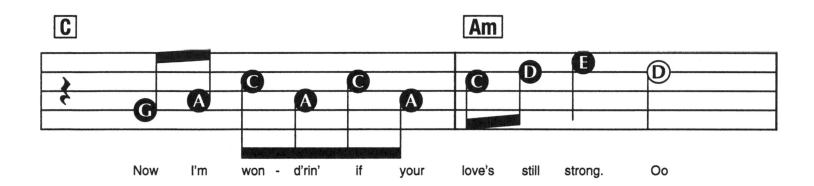

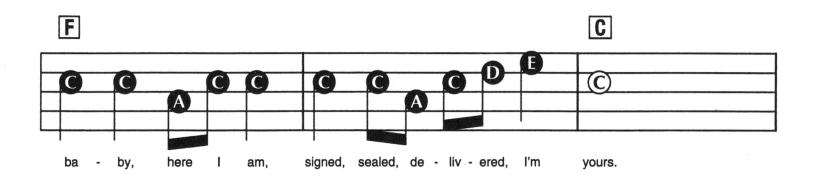

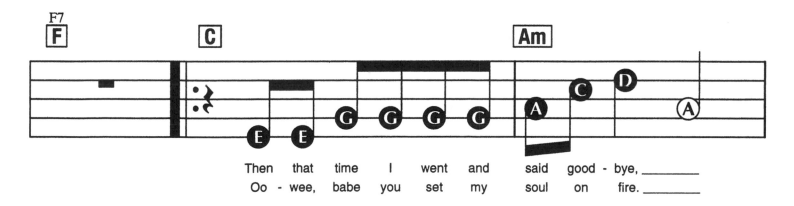

© 1970 (Renewed 1998) JOBETE MUSIC CO., INC., BLACK BULL MUSIC and SAWANDI MUSIC
c/o EMI APRIL MUSIC INC. and EMI BLACKWOOD MUSIC INC.
All Rights Reserved   International Copyright Secured   Used by Permission

60

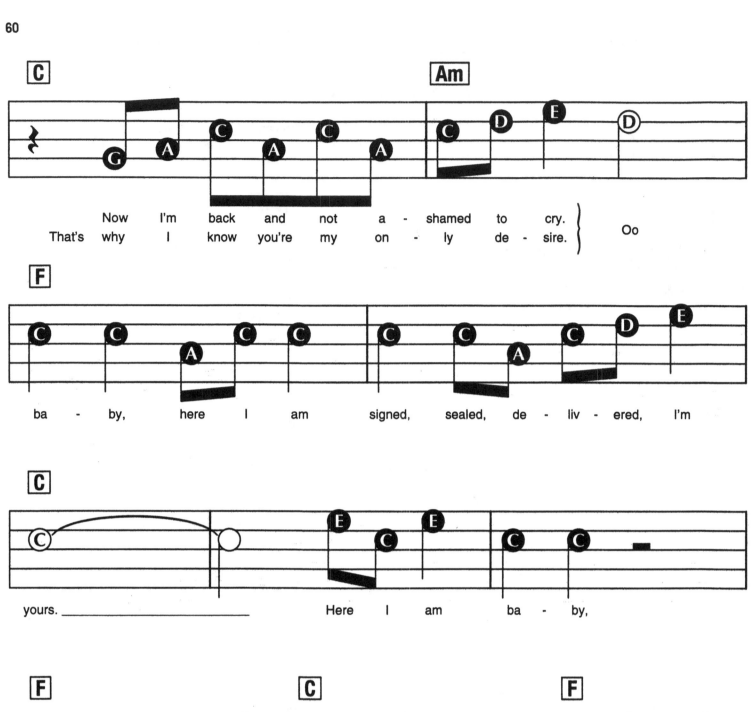

Now I'm back and not a - shamed to cry.
That's why I know you're my on - ly de - sire. } Oo

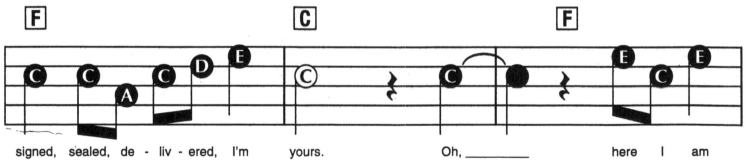

ba - by, here I am signed, sealed, de - liv - ered, I'm

yours. _____ Here I am ba - by,

signed, sealed, de - liv - ered, I'm yours. Oh, _____ here I am

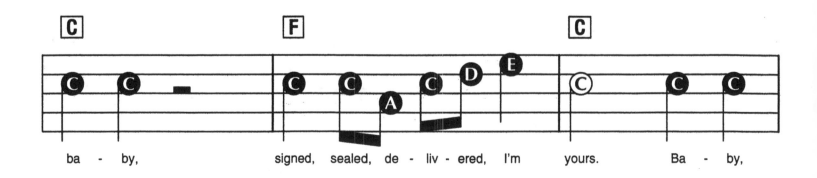

ba - by, signed, sealed, de - liv - ered, I'm yours. Ba - by,

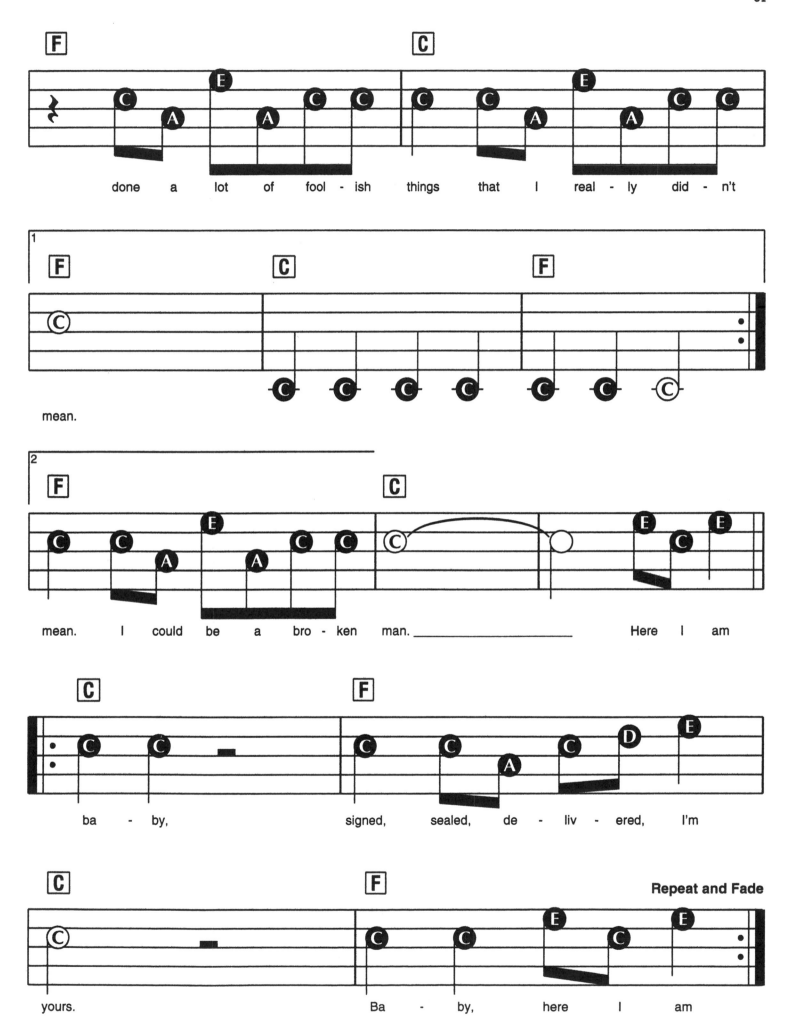

Superstition

Registration 5
Rhythm: Rock or Disco

Words and Music by
Stevie Wonder

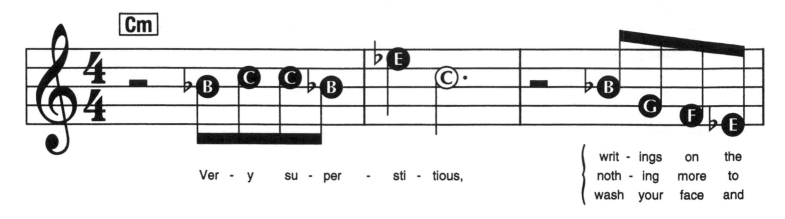

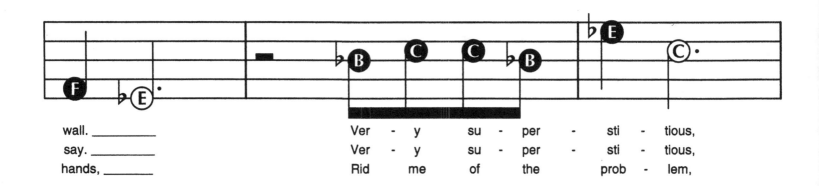

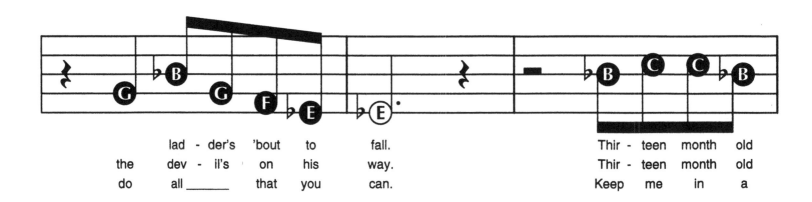

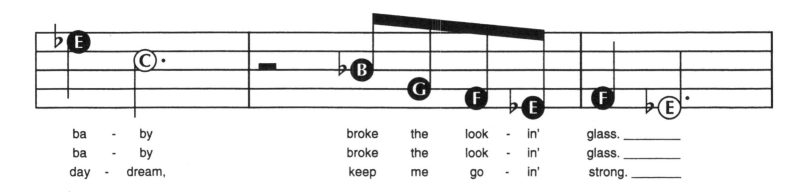

© 1972 (Renewed 2000) JOBETE MUSIC CO., INC. and BLACK BULL MUSIC
c/o.EMI APRIL MUSIC INC.
All Rights Reserved   International Copyright Secured   Used by Permission

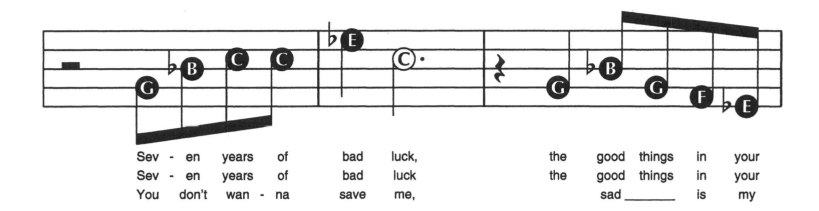

Sev - en years of bad luck, the good things in your
Sev - en years of bad luck the good things in your
You don't wan - na save me, sad _____ is my

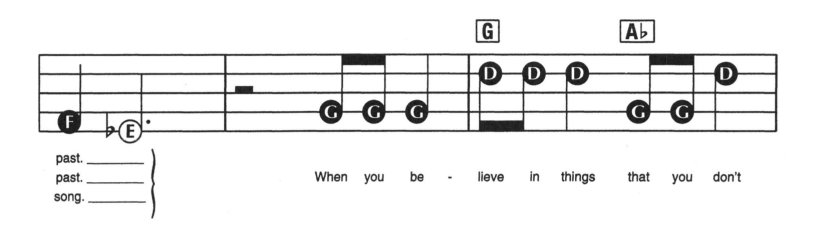

past. _____
past. _____
song. _____

When you be - lieve in things that you don't

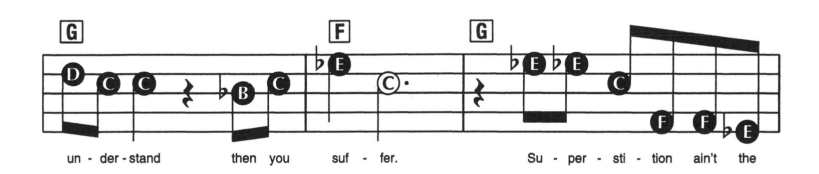

un - der - stand then you suf - fer. Su - per - sti - tion ain't the

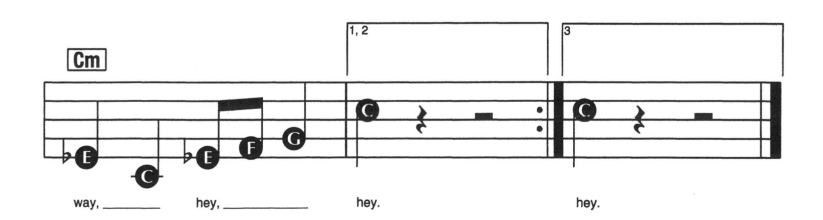

way, _____ hey, _____ hey. hey.

Sir Duke

Registration 9
Rhythm: Rock

Words and Music by
Stevie Wonder

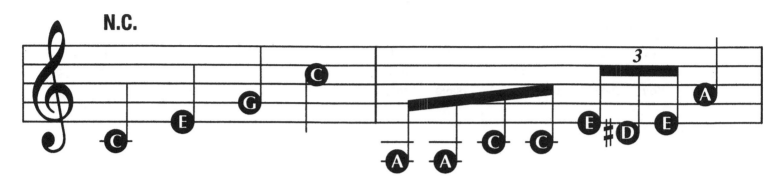

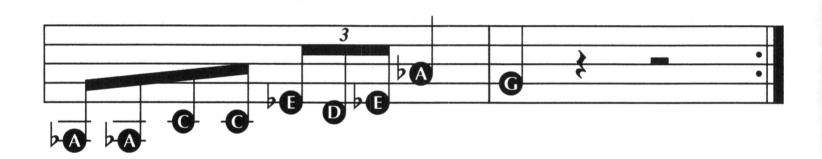

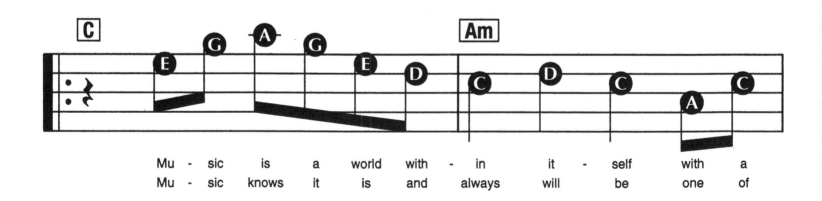

Mu - sic is a world with - in it - self with a
Mu - sic knows it is and al - ways it will be one of

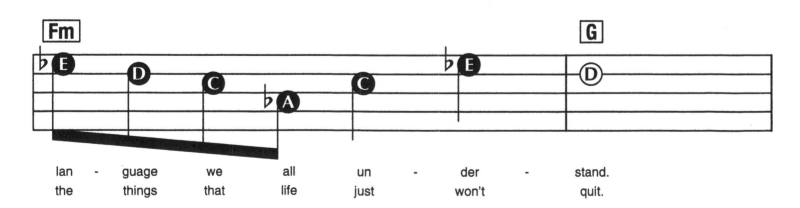

lan - guage we all un - der - stand.
the things that all life just won't quit.

© 1976 JOBETE MUSIC CO., INC. and BLACK BULL MUSIC
c/o EMI APRIL MUSIC INC.
All Rights Reserved   International Copyright Secured   Used by Permission

65

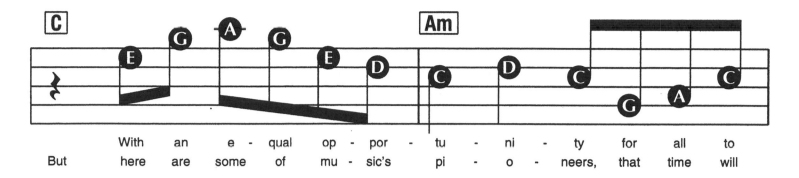

With an e - qual op - por - tu - ni - ty for all to
But here are some of mu - sic's pi - o - neers, that time will

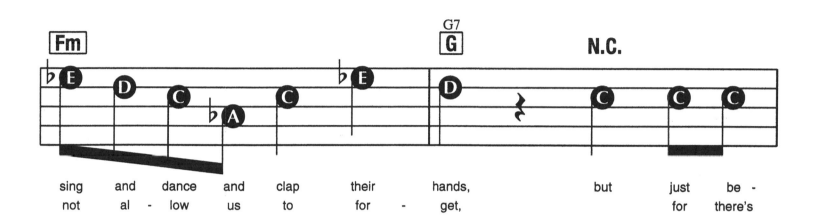

sing and dance and clap their hands, but just be -
not al - low us to for - get, for there's

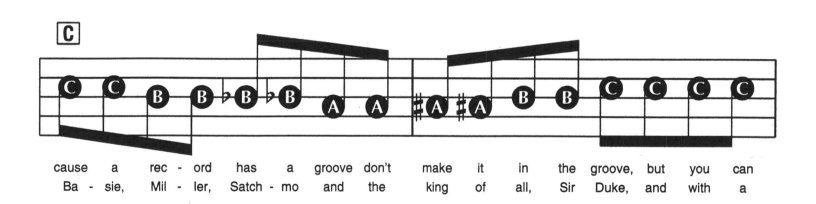

cause a rec - ord has a groove don't make it in the groove, but you can
Ba - sie, Mil - ler, Satch - mo and the king of all, Sir Duke, and with a

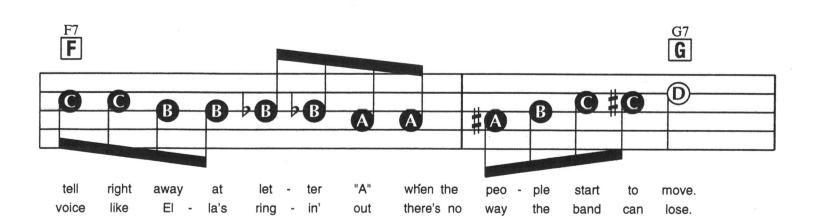

tell right away at let - ter "A" when the peo - ple start to move.
voice like El - la's ring - in' out there's no way the band can lose.

66

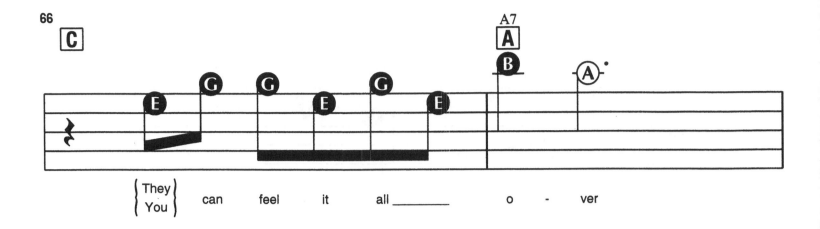

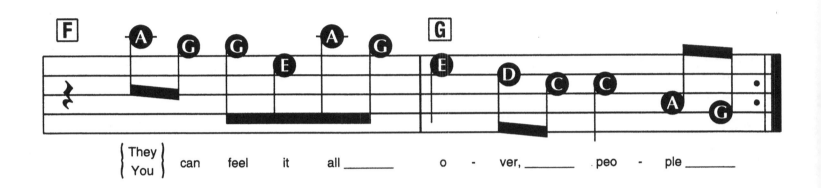

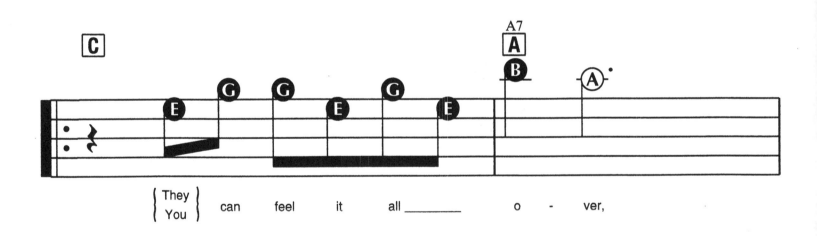

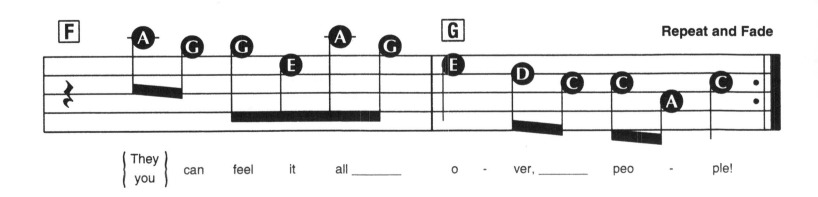

That Girl

Registration 2
Rhythm: Rock

Words and Music by
Stevie Wonder

© 1981 JOBETE MUSIC CO., INC. and BLACK BULL MUSIC
c/o EMI APRIL MUSIC INC.
All Rights Reserved   International Copyright Secured   Used by Permission

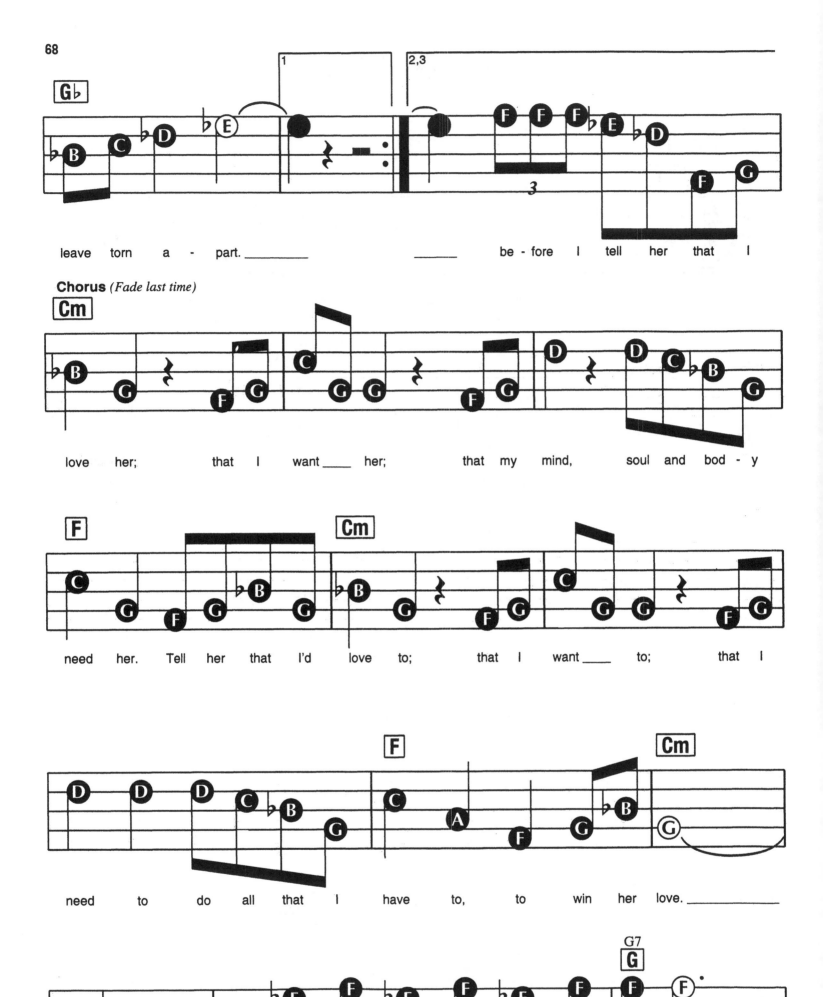

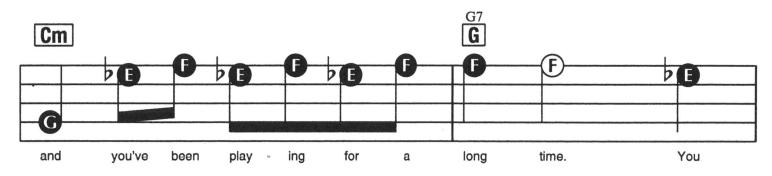

and you've been play - ing for a long time. You

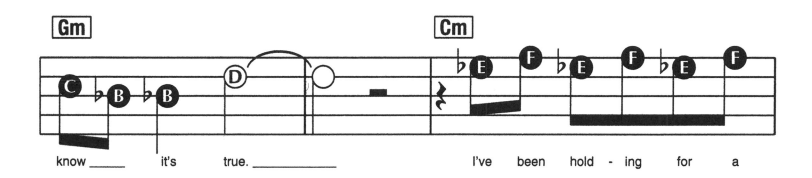

know _____ it's true. _____ I've been hold - ing for a

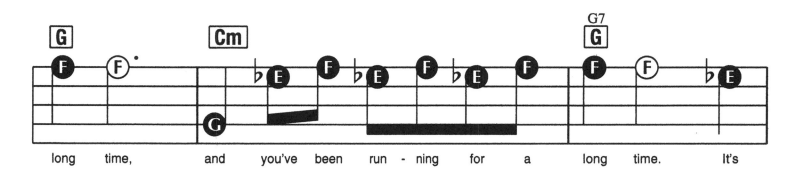

long time, and you've been run - ning for a long time. It's

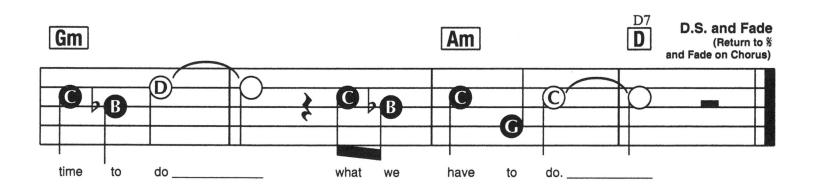

time to do _____ what we have to do. _____

Additional Lyrics

2. That girl thinks that she's so fine,
She'll change my tears to joy from sad.
She says she keeps the upper hand
'Cause she can please her man.
She doesn't use her love to make him weak,
She uses love to keep him strong;
And inside me there's no room for doubt that it won't be too long
Before I tell her that I
Chorus

Uptight
(Everything's Alright)

Registration 8
Rhythm: Rock or 8 - Beat

Words and Music by Stevie Wonder,
Sylvia Moy and Henry Cosby

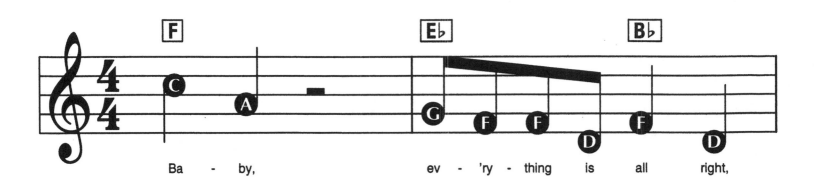

Ba - by, ev - 'ry - thing is all right,

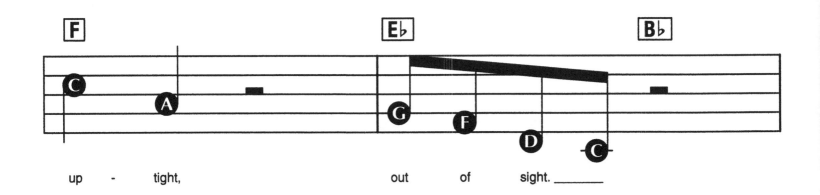

up - tight, out of sight. _____

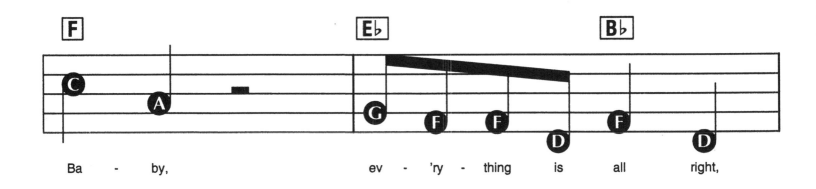

Ba - by, ev - 'ry - thing is all right,

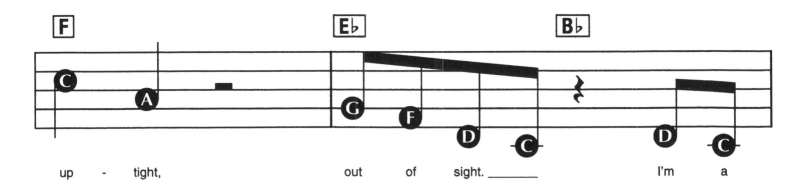

up - tight, out of sight. _____ I'm a

© 1965 (Renewed 1993) JOBETE MUSIC CO., INC., BLACK BULL MUSIC and SAWANDI MUSIC
c/o EMI APRIL MUSIC INC. and EMI BLACKWOOD MUSIC INC.
All Rights Reserved   International Copyright Secured   Used by Permission

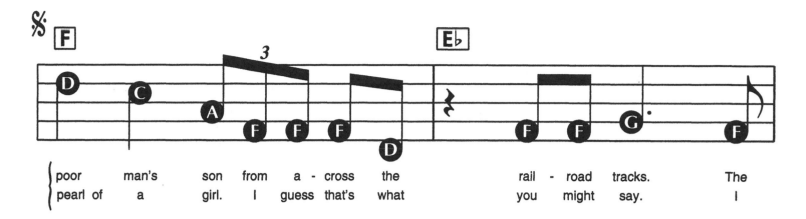

poor man's son from a - cross the   rail - road tracks.   The
pearl of a girl. I guess that's what   you might say.   I

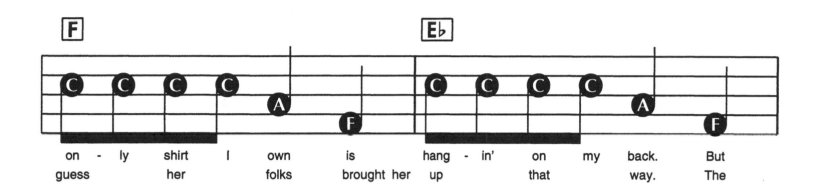

on - ly shirt I own is   hang - in' on my back.   But
guess her folks is brought her up   that way.   The

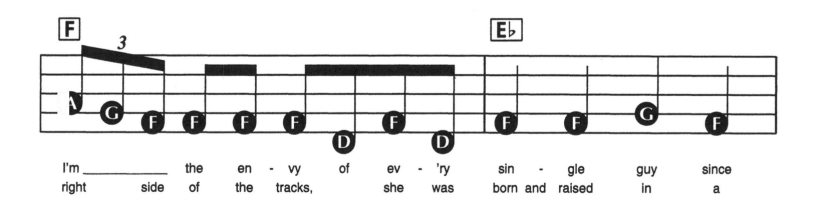

I'm _____ the en - vy of ev - 'ry sin - gle guy since
right side of the tracks, she was born and raised in a

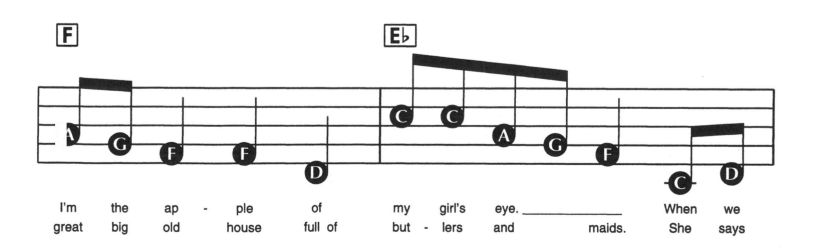

I'm the ap - ple of my girl's eye. _____ When we
great big old house full of but - lers and maids. She says

go out step - ping on the town for a while, my
give her the things that mon - ey can buy, but I'll

mon - ey's low and my suit's out of style. But it's
nev - er nev - er nev - er make my ba - by cry. And it's

all right if my clothes aren't _____ new.
all right what I can't do.

Out of sight be - cause my heart is true. She says
Out of sight be - cause my heart is true. She says

Ba - by, ev - 'ry - thing is all right,

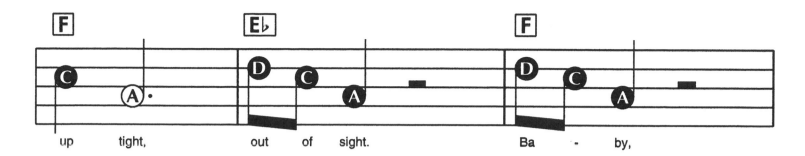

up tight, out of sight. Ba - by,

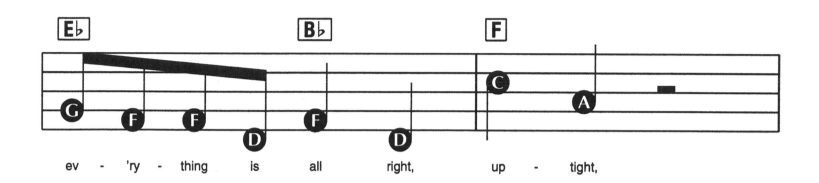

ev - 'ry - thing is all right, up - tight,

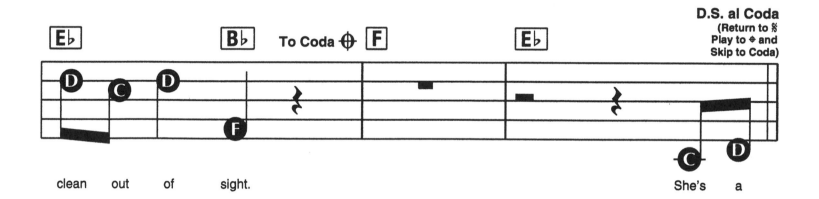

clean out of sight. She's a

CODA

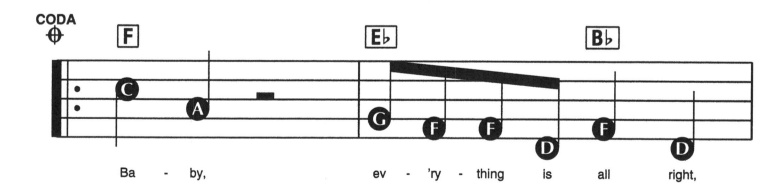

Ba - by, ev - 'ry - thing is all right,

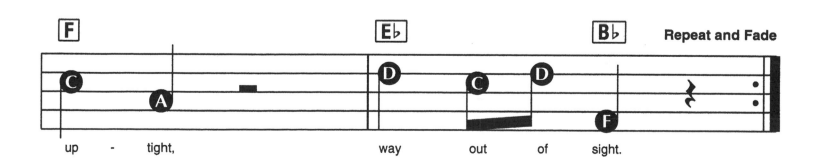

up - tight, way out of sight.

Yester-Me, Yester-You, Yesterday

Registration 4
Rhythm: Rock

Words by Ron Miller
Music by Bryan Wells

© 1966 (Renewed 1994) JOBETE MUSIC CO., INC.
All Rights Controlled and Administered by EMI APRIL MUSIC INC.
All Rights Reserved   International Copyright Secured   Used by Permission

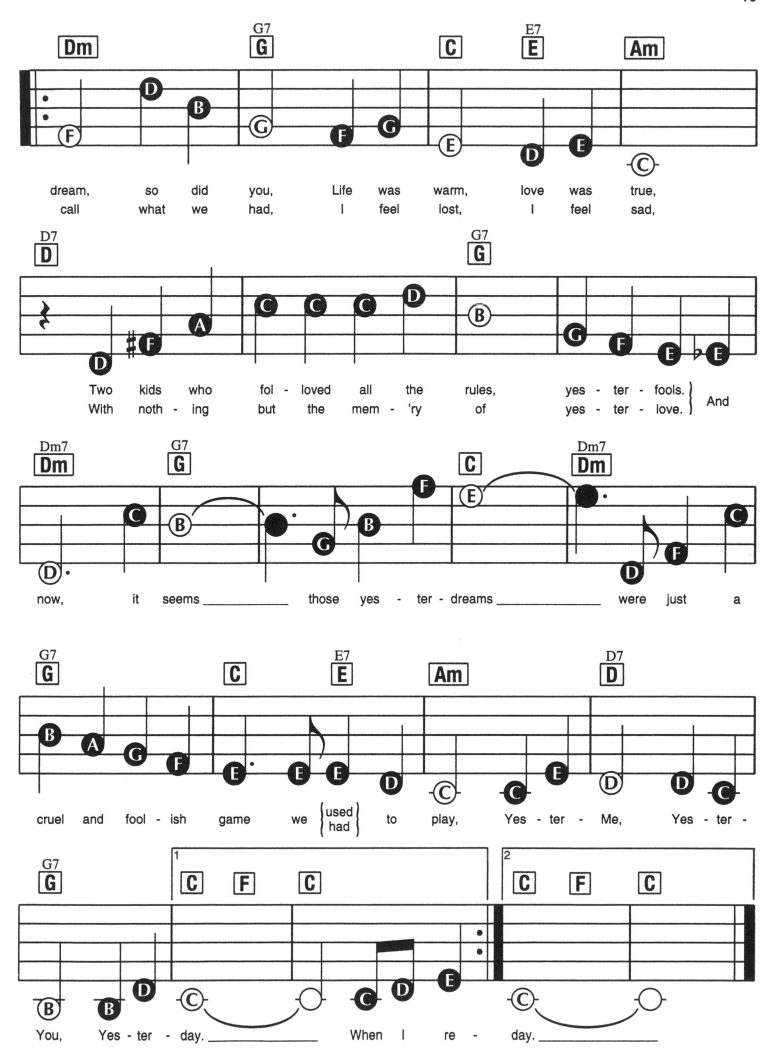

You Are the Sunshine of My Life

Registration 7
Rhythm: 8 Beat or Bossa Nova

Words and Music by
Stevie Wonder

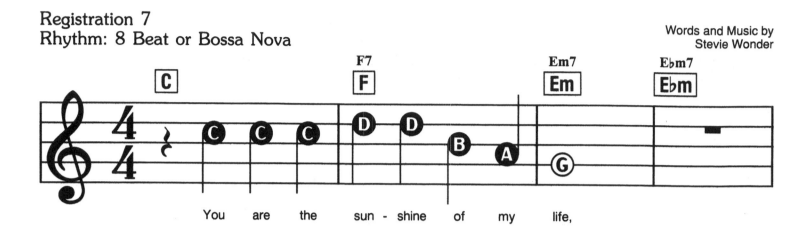

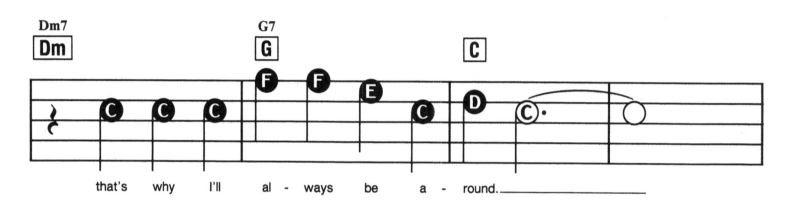

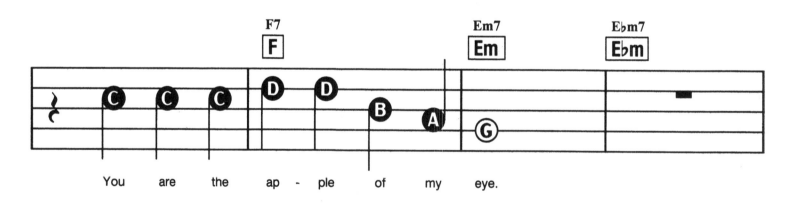

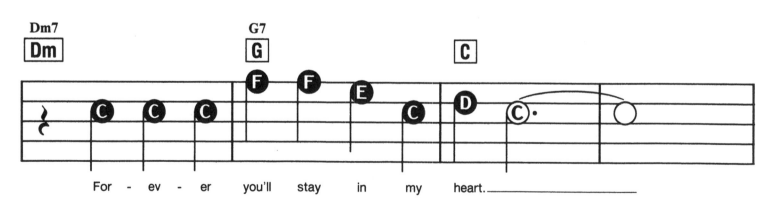

© 1972 (Renewed 2000) JOBETE MUSIC CO., INC. and BLACK BULL MUSIC
c/o EMI APRIL MUSIC INC.
All Rights Reserved   International Copyright Secured   Used by Permission

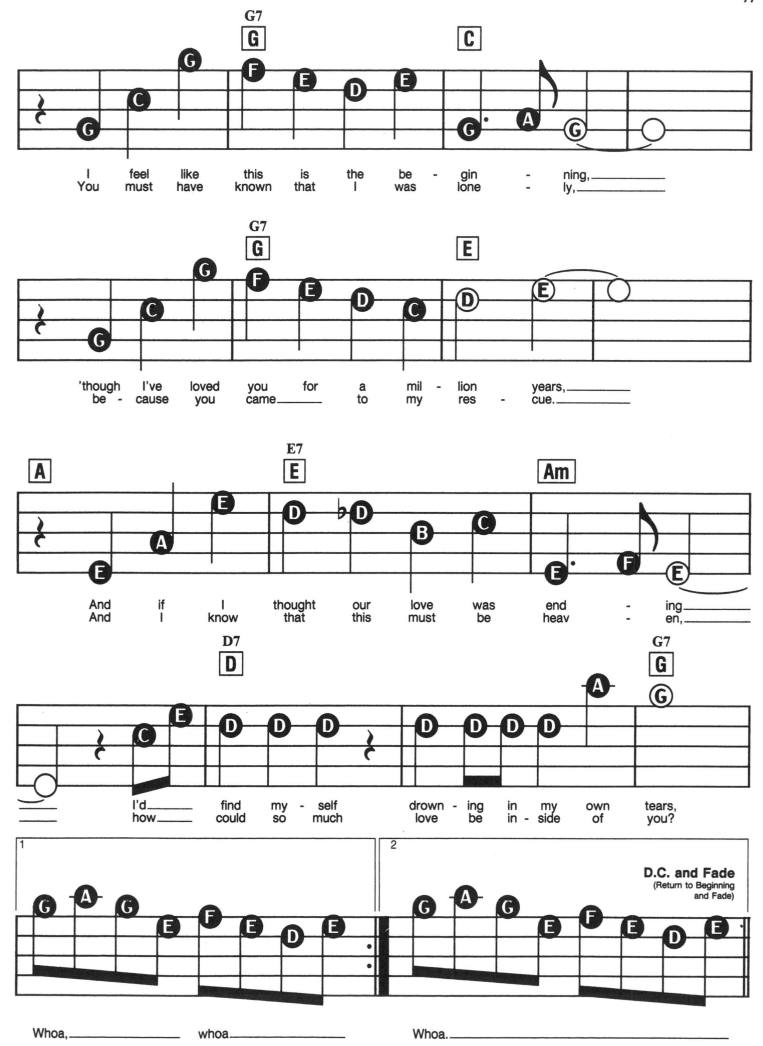

I feel like this is the be - gin - ning,_____
You must have known that I was lone - ly,_____

'though I've loved you for a mil - lion years,_____
be - cause you came_____ to my res - cue._____

And if I thought our love was end - ing_____
And I know that this must be heav - en,_____

I'd_____ find my - self drown - ing in my own tears,
how_____ could so much love be in - side of you?

Whoa,_____ whoa_____

D.C. and Fade
(Return to Beginning and Fade)

Whoa._____

You Haven't Done Nothin'

Registration 8
Rhythm: Rock

Words and Music by
Stevie Wonder

© 1974 (Renewed 2002) JOBETE MUSIC CO., INC. and BLACK BULL MUSIC
c/o EMI APRIL MUSIC INC.
All Rights Reserved   International Copyright Secured   Used by Permission

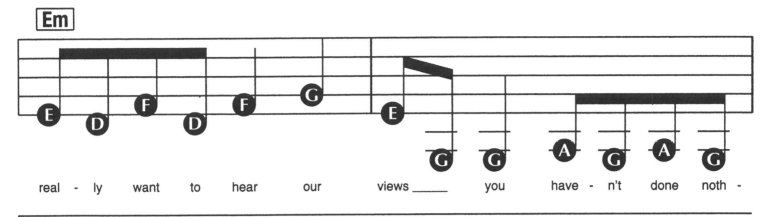

Em

real - ly want to hear our views _____ you have - n't done noth -

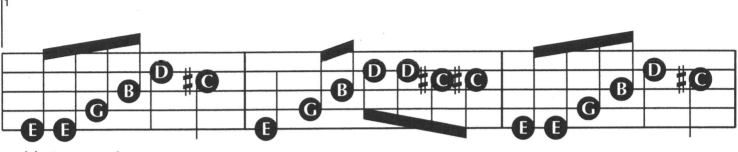

in'. *Instrumental*

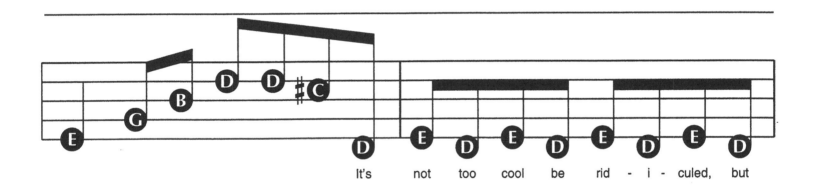

It's not too cool be rid - i - culed, but

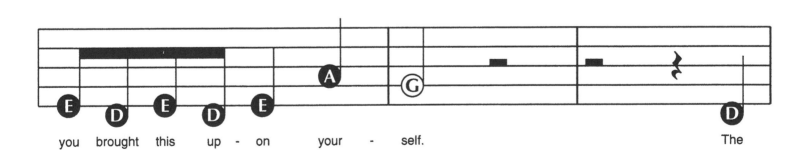

you brought this up - on your - self.   The

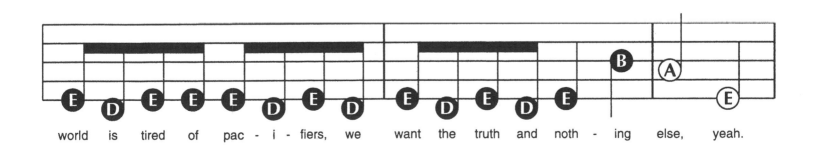

world is tired of pac - i - fiers, we want the truth and noth - ing else, yeah.

80

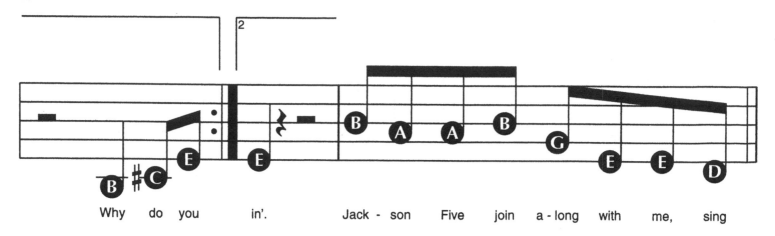

Why do you in'. Jack - son Five join a - long with me, sing

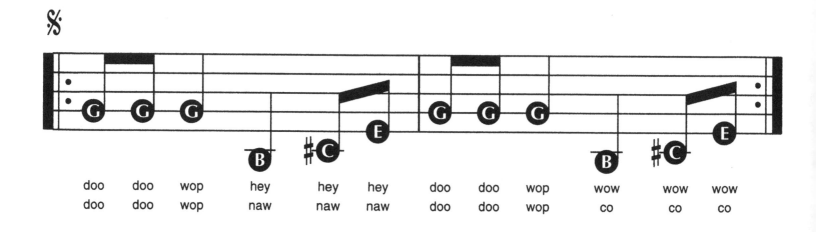

doo doo wop hey hey hey doo doo wop wow wow wow
doo doo wop naw naw naw doo doo wop co co co

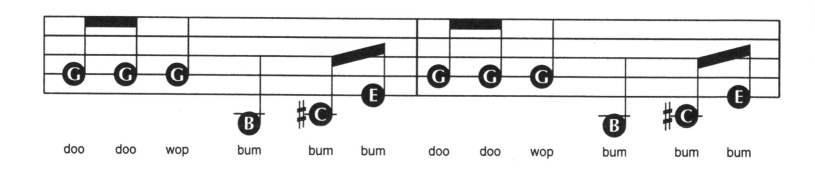

doo doo wop bum bum bum doo doo wop bum bum bum

D.S. and Fade
(Return to 𝄋
and Fade)

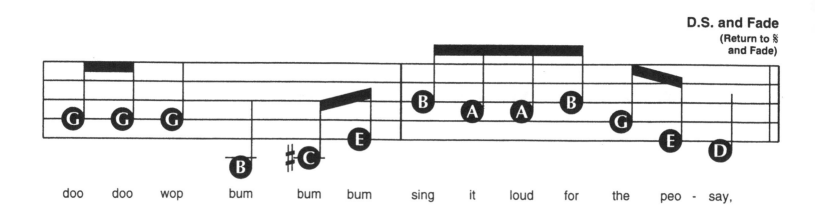

doo doo wop bum bum bum sing it loud for the peo - say,